VIV ANDERSON

# VIV ANDERSON

*by*

ANDREW LONGMORE

HEINEMANN KINGSWOOD

Heinemann Kingswood
Michelin House, 81 Fulham Road, London SW3 6RB
LONDON MELBOURNE AUCKLAND



First published 1988

ISBN 0-434-98153-2

Printed and bound in Great Britain by
Richard Clay Ltd, Bungay, Suffolk

DEDICATIONS

*Viv Anderson:*

To my wife Debra, my mother, father and brother for their support throughout my career.

*Andrew Longmore:*

To my wife Jane and my daughters Anna and Jessica for tolerating my sporting obsession and for making me happy.

# CONTENTS

# ILLUSTRATIONS

# ACKNOWLEDGMENTS

I would like to thank Martin O'Neill, Peter Shilton, Ian Bowyer, Don Howe, John Barnes, Debra Anderson, Mr and Mrs Audley Anderson, Donald Anderson and many others, who gave up their time to answer interminable questions; and Derek Wyatt, Margot Richardson and Tony Pocock, past and present employees of Heinemann Kingswood, who have unfailingly calmed the nerves and boosted the confidence of the first-timer. And, finally, Viv's memory, wherever it is.

The photographs in this book are published by kind permission of Allsport (nos 5, 7, 8, 9, 10, 11 and 13), Bob Thomas (nos 3, 4, and 6), the *Daily Mirror* (no. 12), and Fotosport International (no. 13 inset).

# INTRODUCTION

'The significance?' said Doug Williams of the Washington Redskins, when asked about becoming the first black quarterback to play in the Super Bowl. 'The significance is that we can win it.' Transfer the question and the answer back to November 1978, and you have some idea of Viv Anderson's reaction when he became the first black footballer to play for England.

The truth is that 'significance' questions are often asked but seldom answered, particularly by footballers, who are not prone to deep sociological analysis. And the even simpler truth is that on that frozen night at Wembley, the significance of the occasion for young Anderson was not that he was about to lead a black revolution against the palace of the Football Association at Lancaster Gate but that he was getting a chance to establish himself as a regular international. That he also happened to be the object of national attention was just one of those accidents of history, a case of being in the right place at the right time. Or perhaps the wrong place at the right time, because it is arguably Anderson's misfortune that he will be remembered not for his ability as a footballer, not for his one League Championship, two European Cup and three League Cup medals, not for his thirty or so international caps, but for his colour. Like it or not, when he walked out of the Wembley tunnel to be greeted by a crowd of 92,000 the tall, slim figure was bearing the standard for black people in Britain. Recognition? Yes. A new generation? Yes. Acceptance? Well, it was a start.

If he had been sent off, given away a penalty or scored an own goal, it would have confirmed the belief of householders up and down the country that West Indians were, of course, thoroughly unreliable. Imagine what Alf Garnett would have made of it.

There were plenty of other candidates for the role of black standard-bearer, Laurie Cunningham and Cyrille Regis of West Bromwich Albion being the main ones. Both were brilliant players, but both epitomized the popular perception of the black footballer: fast, lithe and dazzlingly inconsistent. They were flashy players and ever since the days of world heavyweight champion Jack Johnson, who took delight in humiliating his white opponents, the notion of the flashy black sportsman had been viewed with suspicion in Anglo-Saxon eyes. Cunningham once gave the black power salute at the end of a match when he was with his first club, Orient (or Leyton Orient as they have become again). Suspect, very suspect. At that time the 22-year-old Anderson wouldn't have known a black power salute from a handshake. He certainly was not flashy – for a start, he was a full-back. He did not come from a broken home, he was not deprived, he lived with his mum and dad and he also happened to be, in the words of his manager at Nottingham Forest, polite, intelligent, reliable and well brought up. In fact, just like a million middle-class white kids. As England manager Greenwood said: 'I had to take his character into consideration because we expected a little fuss to be made of him.'

At the time, Anderson himself was slightly puzzled by the fuss. One interview he gave, in the *Guardian*, began: 'Viv Anderson's look of mild amusement said it all: why is this reporter going on about Martin Luther King, Muhammad Ali, Pele, ethnic groups and racial prejudice when I'd rather stick to talking about football?' In preparing this book I never did talk to him about Martin Luther King, Muhammad Ali or Pele, but if I had I doubt if the look of mild amusement would have changed. Mild amusement is the way the Anderson family have countered racial prejudice throughout their lives. Besides, the whole point is not just that Anderson has played for England – cricketers Roland Butcher, Norman Cowans and Wilf Slack have all done that and they were born in the West Indies – not just that he regards himself as English, but that, old boy, he actually *is* English: so English that the only time in his life he felt really uncomfortable was when he went to Jamaica at the age of twelve.

Anderson himself has taken that as read from the moment he was born. But it has taken others rather longer to understand.

My first meeting with Viv was in his house in Elstree. The house was neat, new and had the biggest television I had ever seen. There were two cars in the drive and all the trappings of a successful footballer. Anderson was dressed in a Joshua Tree T-shirt and jeans. He was confident, cocky even, and he couldn't keep still. He seemed casual, happy-go-lucky, lazy perhaps, temperamental possibly, unreliable certainly. Typically West Indian, in fact. Subsequent meetings shattered the illusion. He is casual about some things – his colour, above all; he is happy-go-lucky in that he has no plan for life. Things happen, he reacts. He hasn't a clue what he will do when he retires. He admits he is moody, particularly if he loses at anything, but he is definitely not lazy – except, possibly, during training – or unreliable. In fact, he possesses some classic English characteristics: reserve, thrift, caution, determination, and far from being confident or arrogant, he is even a little shy. The two biggest ordeals of his life have been personal, not professional. The first was being best man to Tony Woodcock, the second was getting married himself, which he did without telling his parents.

But, above all that, the most striking thing about Anderson is his unbridled enthusiasm for the game of soccer. Even now, at the age of thirty-two, when the end of his career beckons, when injuries do not heal quite so quickly, when nasty youthful wingers take it upon themselves to test the battleworn limbs of the veteran, he has the same raw energy as when he first started back in 1974. And he still has a fair turn of pace, despite his wonky knees. As the Manchester United manager Alex Ferguson said: 'When you think of all that he has done in the game his enthusiasm is remarkable. You can't buy that.' He did, of course, for £250,000 in the summer of 1987. But you know what he means. Not many players can open their trophy cabinet and have a total of six championship and cup medals come tumbling out. Even fewer can claim that their careers actually progressed – at least in financial terms – after such success. Forest to Arsenal to Manchester United. Most players would be happy with any one of them.

When I asked Anderson why he wanted to do a book, his reply was instinctive and revealing: 'So that I can give it to my mother.' But I can understand why he said it. Viv's mother is a formidable woman with fiery eyes and a temper to match. Though she never actively discouraged it, she never wanted her son to be a professional footballer. She wanted him to get a proper job, to be a teacher or an accountant. She still gets worried that he won't make it. This book is the proof that he did.

ONE

# 'YELLOW, PURPLE OR BLACK'

The England manager, Ron Greenwood, announcing his team for the match against Czechoslovakia, said, 'Yellow, purple or black – if they're good enough, I'll pick them.' In the absence in the Football League at that time of any purples or yellows, the reference was fairly clear. On 29 November 1978, eleven men wearing England shirts would appear out of the Wembley tunnel, ten of them white and one black. It would, added Greenwood, be a 'little bit of history', which is why the name of Viv Anderson will be remembered in the textbooks long after far greater footballers have been consigned to the shelf marked 'football statistics'.

In choosing Anderson, Greenwood was expressing an important belief: that sport, and particularly football, should be one area of society where no consideration is given to race, colour or creed. Racial prejudice is still rife in football, but on the terraces not in the dressing-room, where winning is all that matters. As Ron Greenwood's successor as England manager, Bobby Robson, once said: 'If the eleven best players in the country were all black, they'd all play.' Viv himself has put his hand on his heart and, with just a moment's hesitation, said that never in his career has he felt that his colour has been a factor in his selection for a team. 'It would shatter my illusions completely if I ever thought that was the case,' he added.

But just as sport likes to see itself as an oasis of equal opportunity, it is also one of the sharpest pins with which to prick the conscience and prejudice of a nation. Certainly, the Commission for Racial Equality was not slow to exploit the unaccustomed attention given to a black footballer. 'The more blacks can get involved in mainstream activities like football and other sports, and be selected on merit, the more people will see them as part and parcel of the British game,' said a spokesman for the Commission when the England squad was announced a week before the match. The Commission might have added 'the more people will see them as part and parcel of British society', but perhaps they felt that such sentiments would be too optimistic. Notice, though, the word 'merit'. How else do you select a team?

The press were not likely to miss such an opportunity either. For weeks beforehand they had been having fun, guessing who the first black player would be. Cunningham and Regis were the favourites. Anderson's case too had been advanced in the newspapers, which have a hypnotic influence on these things, whatever managers may say. The announcement of the England B squad, which included Cunningham and Regis but not Anderson, a few days before the full team, heightened speculation that Anderson would get his first cap. But on the day the squad was announced he was told the news of his inclusion by a local journalist and thought it was a joke. A few minutes later he heard it on the radio and rushed to the City Ground to open the letter which confirmed it.

Though Greenwood had suggested that he would be playing, Anderson did not know for certain. He was given a day off by Forest to give interviews, but not wanting to tempt fate he had to keep saying: 'If it happens . . .' During the week leading up to the game, Viv had more words written about him than in all the previous four years of his professional career. His mum, his dad, his aunts, uncles and brother became celebrities overnight. BBC and ITV vied with each other to get their interviews with the family. There was not enough room for all the camera crews and their equipment in the comfortable but small semi-detached house on a housing estate in Clifton in Nottingham where Viv had been brought up. Yes, said his parents, they were very proud of Viv. Yes, he had always wanted to play for England. Yes, he was 'over the moon'. All the usual mundanity on which football thrives. The difference between those answers and many of the others that are trotted out week after week by managers, players, coaches and chairmen was that they were substantially true, not just automatic answers to elementary questions.

What the interviewers found was that Anderson did not fit into the cosy stereotype of the black in Britain. If he had not been a professional footballer, he would not have been a professional agitator, a layabout, or inhabitant of the local unemployment office. He would have been a printer, plain and simple.

As he came out for his international debut, his thoughts were not of the thousands of black kids who might be inspired by him, but of making sure his winger did not score a hat-trick. At the far back of his mind, though, might have been the vague notion that his appearance represented something wider, something more profound than merely kicking a bag of wind around for ninety minutes, for after all, no one else in the dressing-room had received telegrams from Elton John or Laurie Cunningham's mother wishing them luck.

Audley Anderson, Viv's father – he answers mainly to 'Andy' – had seen more of British society's double standards than his son. Having arrived in Britain from Jamaica in the mid-1950s, the realities of the so-called 'promised land' had hit him hard. The last seat on the bus always the one next to him, the woman with the child walking across the street to avoid going past him, the overtime which he strangely never seemed to get; all the little niggly things that made you feel not quite an outcast, but not exactly one of the boys either. Now here was his first-born son representing that country. In the north stand, just by the royal box at Wembley Stadium, in the enclosure for players' families, people were not shying away from him, but actively seeking him out and congratulating him, while back in the Nottingham hospital where she worked as a nurse similar and unaccustomed attention was being accorded Mrs Myrtle Anderson – or Viv's mum, as she unwillingly became known. Both could be forgiven a wry smile as the national anthem of their adopted homeland heralded the first kick by a black footballer in a senior England shirt. Acceptance, at last, through the sporting talent of a son.

Viv's father had travelled down from Nottingham that afternoon with a friend from work. The television cameras, ready to bleed the moment for every ounce of publicity, had filmed him climbing into his Caravette outside number 121 Rivergreen at the start of the journey. Mrs Anderson would have gone too, though she is not a regular spectator, but the night rota for the men's surgical ward at Highbury Hospital in Nottingham had not been drawn up with the forthcoming international in mind and she was on duty. Unlike a later occasion when he got lost in the rabbit-warren of stairways and passages that lie under the outwardly serene and imperial face of Britain's national football stadium, Andy navigated his way to Turnstile F, Entrance 81, Row 8, Seat 14, without trouble. Outside the ground he had been surrounded by white fans wanting to congratulate him on Viv's selection. 'It made me feel ten feet tall,' he said at the time, but ten years later he finds it hard to describe the match or the occasion. He shifts uneasily in his seat at the thought, knowing perhaps that he can never adequately translate into words the mixed emotions of that night, but he speaks with homespun wisdom, delivered in a tone which is half West Indian lilt, half Nottingham drawl.

'I am not an excitable person, so outwardly I took it all very calmly.

Sometimes you keep things inside that you don't let out. I was very proud – it's a feeling every parent wants to have – because I knew what he had gone through to get there. I was the first black employee at the hospital where I worked and the first one when I moved to Securicor. After two years at the hospital another black man arrived and he said that if he had found it hard at first, it must have been doubly hard for me. Viv was the same.

'You have to be a bit special to be the first one. If you know that when you are wrong you are going to be doubly wrong then you have to try that much harder to be right. It's something you live with all the time; when you go to matches 99 per cent of the crowd is white, when you go on holiday you're the only black person on the plane, the only one in the hotel. You feel that if anything should happen, you're on your own. But Viv's selection helped to uplift the coloured population because it made them see that the gaps between black and white were being closed and that we are just as good as anyone else. That night people who I had never seen before in my life were waving to me because they knew I was Viv's father. It's like life; if you win, you get accepted, if you lose, nobody wants to know.'

From a footballing point of view, Anderson made a more than useful debut on a tricky frozen pitch against a lively Czech side, who defended well and broke quickly. His initial nervousness must have been eased by the familiar faces of his two Forest club colleagues, Peter Shilton and Tony Woodcock, the latter making only his second international appearance. If he could have picked two accomplices for that night, he would have looked no further than those two. Ten years later, Shilton is as permanent a figure in England's goal as Mrs Thatcher is in Downing Street, but he was still understudy to Liverpool's Ray Clemence at that time and as anxious as anyone to prove himself the Number One. A big bear of a man, Shilton has an infectious arrogance most useful when you are a little anxious about your own confidence in the presence of supposedly the best footballers in the land. Shilton, Anderson . . . the pair had appeared so often together in the Forest defence which had conceded only twenty-four league goals throughout the previous season that it seemed only natural they should be the first two on England's team sheet as well. And Woodcock. Woody? Soft-spoken, articulate, and the best friend Viv has in the game. They had come up through Forest's youth team together, broken through into the first team almost together, suffered Clough together, won medals together. Now they were playing for

England together. Woody has a friendly face anyway, but it must have seemed doubly so in the spacious but unwelcoming dressing-rooms of Wembley with 92,000 people waiting outside.

Woodcock recalls that on the days leading up to the game and on the day itself Anderson had been showered with telephone calls and telegrams wishing him well. It had caused an unusually severe bout of barracking in the Forest dressing-room. 'Here comes the history-maker' was the phrase of the week as the Forest players found a novel outlet for the sarcasm and general insensitivity which is the trademark of all sporting dressing-rooms. 'I think it did begin to affect him a bit,' says Woodcock, 'but Viv is not one to show it.' Affected or not, the history-maker made a pretty reasonable debut in an undistinguished England performance, as *The Times* recorded: 'Apart from a swerving shot that Currie spun round the goalpoast, England managed few dangerous moments . . . Indeed one's attention was drawn to the fact that only Anderson was displaying true club form at international level – the criterion of a good player in Mr Greenwood's mind.' To complete a highly satisfactory night, Anderson initiated the only goal of the game, striding forward with the characteristic knees-up style that suggests he is skipping over unseen trip wires before giving the ball to Tony Currie. Currie's low cross into the goalmouth eluded the Czech goalkeeper and a defender, and the dependable Steve Coppell rolled the ball over the line to give England a welcome and slightly fortunate victory. If, in American terms, it could not quite be termed 'an assist', Anderson's involvement in the match-winning move provided Fleet Street with just the excuse they needed to pick out the young coloured full-back as one of the stars of the night, thereby justifying their pushing of him in the first place.

After the match, Greenwood made all the right noises – 'settled down well', 'very pleased with him', and so on. Viv managed to snatch a few words with his father before going back to the hotel, and Mr Anderson turned his Caravette towards the north and drove home through the fog. History had been made; except for one unfortunate sequel. On the following morning, Viv's mother was injured in a car crash as she was driving to work. She suffered severe facial injuries and, instead of going to her hospital as a nurse, went in as a patient.

If Anderson's selection that night was supposed to herald a black revolution in the game, it was a long time coming. Phil Neal returned for four of the next five internationals; Trevor Cherry played in the other. Laurie Cunningham duly made his international debut against

Wales at Wembley early that summer, but only played twice more for England, and Cyrille Regis had to wait another three years to become the third coloured England international when he made his full debut in the unlikely surroundings of Reykjavik in the summer of 1982. There were plenty of players on the fringes of international selection – Garth Crooks, Vince Hilaire, Garry Thompson and Ricky Hill, for example – but, of those, only Hill graduated to the top level. As for Anderson, 'the history-maker' had to wait until 10 June 1979 to prove himself again, a gap that hurt his professional far more than his racial pride.

TWO

# THE PROMISED LAND

Winston Churchill was Prime Minister and Chelsea were on course to win the championship (the only time they have done so) when, in October 1954, a small thickset man with a deep bass voice arrived in Plymouth on a boat from Jamaica, a few addresses in his pocket. For Audley Anderson, as for 9000 other West Indians that year, Britain offered a new life. If not exactly the land of milk and honey, then at least a land where you could find a job, decent accommodation and, above all, peace. Few really expected much more than that. Certainly not Anderson, who is not a man given to flights of fancy.

At the time, the number of West Indian immigrants to Britain was a trickle compared to the full flow of the early 1960s. The Conservative government had no firm policy on immigration, leaving the social welfare of the new settlers to voluntary organizations. It was not until 1962 that under pressure from the rapid rise in immigration figures the government passed the Commonwealth Immigration Act, which tightened up the regulations on immigration from Commonwealth countries. There was, however, a dimly perceived notion that large communities of black people settling in inner cities could cause problems. Sometimes this took the form of a call for restriction, as in a minute by J. B. Wilson, Under-Secretary of State at the Colonial Office in 1950. 'We are convinced that it is very greatly to the detriment of the Colonial peoples themselves that this influx should continue,' he wrote. 'We see no prospect that if it does continue we can avoid the creation of serious social problems such as the growth of depressed coloured quarters in English cities and a considerable increase in colour feeling on the part of the general population.'

This was, in one way, a typical attitude, and in another quite extreme. The feeling that restriction was in the interests of the newcomers themselves was a typical politician's response to a problem. Less typical, though, was the strong recognition that there were social problems inherent in continued unrestricted immigration. For the most part, the government ignored such warnings. Local social services were left to cope as best they could pursuing an *ad hoc* policy which can be most usefully described as 'shuffle and deal': one for Birmingham, one for Nottingham, one for London. It might have been crude, but it seemed in the short term at least to be reasonably effective. When I asked Mrs Anderson, who followed her husband to England in February 1955, why they had chosen Nottingham to live, she had replied: 'I think Andy just put a pin in a map. I really don't know.' Actually, the answer was even simpler than that. The Andersons were dealt out to Nottingham.

In retrospect, it was not a bad card to be given. There was work in the city and, though there was a growing West Indian population, there was not the tension that was experienced in London. After a day of rioting in 1958 in the district just to the north of where the Andersons were living (an unplanned reaction to a pub fight rather than an outbreak of long-term dissatisfaction), newcomers and citizens agreed to live side by side in peace if not complete harmony. Anderson recalls: 'I liked Nottingham when I first arrived and I still like it. I regard myself as a Nottingham person now. I remember arriving at the big old station for the first time and then going to see the local welfare people set up to help immigrants from the West Indies find accommodation and work. Of course, we were a bit different because the majority had somewhere to go. We had nothing. I had a few addresses – Leeds, Birmingham maybe – but I wanted to find my own way and not rely on anyone else.'

That streak of independence was not new. Three years earlier Anderson had already forsaken the warmth and comfort of his father's smallholdings in the parish of St Catherine's, east of Kingston, to go to America. His father owned three farms, two of five acres and one of three, on which he grew a variety of crops and fruit: cocoa, sugar cane, bananas, coffee. He also owned a small sugar mill. Audley was one of seven children, and the only boy. After going to the local school, he went to agricultural college presumably in the expectation that he would work on his father's land and eventually take over. But that was not his idea of a good life. Perhaps having three elder sisters and three younger had something to do with it; perhaps it was the tales of profit and paradise told by friends coming back after the war; perhaps it was just itchy feet. Whatever it was, he took off to Connecticut to work a three-year contract on a tobacco farm. There he earned enough money to save, but, above all, he learnt. He learnt about the techniques of tobacco farming, which did not prove any use to him at all during the rest of his life, and he learnt about racial prejudice, which did.

'In America, it is worse than it is here. I was working with lots of Polish people, displaced persons, and there was segregation. You couldn't eat at the same table as the whites, you couldn't go through the same door. I saw those sort of things, so it was easier for me coming to England than it might have been for someone who came straight here from the West Indies. Lines were more strongly drawn in America then. In America they say "stay over there", and that's it. In England, they don't actually say that, but you can feel the resentment if you don't.'

After three years he went back to Jamaica, but could not settle. He might have gone back to the States, though his contract was not renewed, or he could have stayed. Instead he made the decision, like countless school friends, to come to England. 'The kind of life in Jamaica didn't suit me. At first, Jamaica was like a paradise, but when people started going away and seeing other places for themselves during the war, it was never quite the same. There was increased violence at the time, political violence, and the more people went away and came back again, the worse the violence got. There was not much work at the time, and besides everyone wants better. Everyone wants to know what's on the other side of the fence. So we decided to come here,' said Anderson.

The 'we', by the middle of 1954, referred to his new wife, a local girl from St Catherine's whom he had known for several years. They were married shortly after his return from America and not long after decided to emigrate to England. He was twenty-five, she was twenty-two. Even after thirty-four years, it is clear that the decision had little to do with her. She had to come because duty and love called, but she does not pretend that leaving her family to go to a city which had almost as many inhabitants as the whole of Jamaica was anything other than terrifying. Arriving in the bleak depths of February, she found Nottingham cold and forbidding and the people equally so. For her, Nottingham was not A. L. Rowse's 'magnificent city full of improbable splendours'. Even now the splendours of Nottingham elude her; on bad days her home, her culture and many of her thoughts are back in St Catherine's where the sun shines all the time and the taps drip pina colada. It did not help that the teacher-training exams she had passed back in Jamaica were not recognized in England so that if she wanted to fulfil her ambition of being a teacher she would have to retake them. It was an early and heavy blow to morale.

'I often ask myself why I decided to come. Where we were in

Jamaica there were miles of space and lots of sunshine. We were a big family and very close. I missed being with my family very much. It was heart-rending. I cried for the first three years and, looking back, I don't know how I survived,' she recalled. Even allowing for an absence of thirty-four years making the heart grow fonder, that is a soulful testament to the loneliness of countless immigrant wives the length and breadth of the country. It was a wonder that parts of Britain's cities did not float away on a tide of Caribbean tears.

After a few months of living in rented accommodation without baths and without much heat, the Andersons moved into a terraced house in Gordon Street to the north of the city. Andy had managed to get a job as a porter in the general hospital – at £6 for a 48-hour week – and their lives had taken on an air of stability which has stayed with them. Andy still works at the hospital, though now as a security officer rather than a porter, and the family have only ever lived in two houses, Gordon Road and Rivergreen on the Clifton Estate, at one time reputed to be the largest housing estate in Europe. Even that move was forced on them when the council bought their house in Gordon Road.

Stability is important to the Anderson family. Both parents had it in their own family lives and they were determined that they should pass it on to their own children. Viv has been lucky in that he has benefited from that attitude not only in the way his own career has developed but in his own outwardly casual but inwardly cautious approach to life.

When he was born on 29 July 1956 Vivian Alexander Anderson, named after one of Andy's close school friends, was spindly, weak and sickly, only 5 lb 9 oz at birth and scarcely increasing his weight over the next nine months. Psychologists would say that the health of the boy reflected the mental state of the mother. Perhaps so, but there was a dramatic improvement in both during the next few years as Viv grew upward if not much outward and found solace in kicking a football endlessly around the backyard in Gordon Road, dressed usually in hat, gloves and thick jacket to ward off the cold. It later became a standing joke in the family that Viv could never play professional football because he would get too cold and wet. In that sense, he was his mother's son.

Partly because his progress through school and childhood was quite normal, but mainly because Viv's own memory is so appalling, the course of his youth has to be put together from fragments rather like an ancient manuscript. But there is one advantage to this selective amnesia: if Viv remembers something, it must be significant. The method is less productive for charting his football career. He will forget crucial European Cup ties, but have total recall about a sodden day at Sunderland. Why? Because he happened to score.

What Viv remembers about his youth is doing as little schoolwork as his teachers and his mother would allow, and playing sport. With his long legs and his pace, which he inherited from his mother's side of the family, he was a natural long-jumper and a good all-round athlete. He pleased his father by playing a bit of cricket, but mainly stuck to soccer, where he was a fast and effective centre-forward. 'I was just taller and quicker than anyone else, so they would knock it up to the front and I'd chase it. I suppose it was the natural position for me to play.' Physically, even culturally, he should by rights have been a cricketer. He is built far more like the classic, lithe West Indian fast bowler than the heavy-thighed, muscular English footballer, but, true to back-street tradition, he automatically turned to football. He cannot say why – if he could, cricket's administrators would pay him a fortune – but it was not an isolated case; while Anderson was honing his footballing skills against the back wall, other black youths with names like Blissett, Chamberlain and Fashanu were doing the same in different parts of the country. In contrast, the first black cricketers to play for England (apart from Basil D'Oliveira who was a Cape Coloured) were still learning their trade on the hard and dusty wickets of their native lands. Whether because of social patterns in England or simply because cricketers tend to take longer than footballers to be selected for their country, cricket has always been a beat behind football in developing coloured talent. It was just under two and a half years after Anderson's England debut that Roland Butcher of Middlesex became the first West Indian-born cricketer to play for England; a further eight before David Lawrence became the first English-born coloured cricketer to play for his country, in the summer of 1988.

Apart from his natural prowess on the sports field, Anderson's childhood is remarkable only for its ordinariness. As long as there was a ball at his feet and a wall to kick it at, he was happy. 'I actually quite enjoyed school. I wasn't all that good at work. Everything revolved around sport. You've heard that a million times before, but it happened to be true. I used to play cricket, football, basketball, athletics, the lot. Surprisingly, I quite liked art too, though I was never particularly good. My mother, being a teacher back in Jamaica, was very aware that I ought to get some qualifications behind me and, of course, she was right. She was always going on at me about it, but it just went in one ear and out the other.'

From the Bluebell Infants school in the north of Nottingham – 'it was an old building, supposed to be haunted, but they knocked it down' – through Greencroft Middle school to Fairham Comprehensive, a massive school on the Clifton Estate, Viv's sport and his ready smile were his main assets, as his former PE master at Fairham, Chris Perry, confirmed. 'He was a good all-rounder, never an academic, but a tremendous triple-jumper, quite a fair cricketer, and his ability as a sprinter still shows in his game. Even at eleven he showed talent, though it is hard to know if a child will maintain that promise. Viv did. Though there were very few black children in the school then, everyone liked Viv because he laughed and smiled so much. It's as simple as that.'

Only occasionally did the fact that his colour might matter cloud his carefree horizon. 'I had a fight with one lad in the playground because he called me something to do with my colour, but generally it didn't cross my mind. I was born and bred in Nottingham just the same as most of the others, so I didn't really think about it. I certainly never got very worked up about it. Perhaps it was because I was bigger than most of the other boys so they didn't pick on me, and obviously my sport helped too.' Getting through school with just one dust-up in the playground is not a bad disciplinary record for any schoolboy, but for a black boy in a predominantly white neighbourhood? Very disappointing for the sociologist – and the black activist. Perhaps it's that selective amnesia again. Or maybe it was just that all his energies were concentrated on playing football and not on contemplating the colour of his navel. School match Saturday morning, Clifton Athletic Saturday afternoon, Mallorca FC Sunday morning – that was the pattern of Anderson's weekend, and if it had been possible he would have played Sunday afternoon as well.

From a relatively early age, Viv learnt that there were two ways of coping with the attitudes of other people towards race. You either fought it or you accepted it. Consciously or subconsciously, he has adopted the latter approach, following his parents in regarding racial prejudice with mild amusement and complete disdain, a reflection of the ignorance of the giver not the inadequacy of the receiver. The black civil rights movement would not have thrived on that sort of nonchalance but, in a working-class profession like football, it has stood Anderson in good stead. He knows as well as anyone that if he had spent his time worrying about the taunts of the crowd or trying to kick someone for making a remark, he would not have lasted long in the game. Mind you, it doesn't stop him from having a dig back once in a while.

Besides, the Anderson family had another problem to cope with. Two years after Viv was born, Myrtle Anderson had another son, Donald. He was a much stronger and healthier infant than his elder brother had been until at the age of two he contracted polio. After months of uncertainty, Donald survived but the strain on the family must have been enormous. Even to this day, the causes of the illness are unclear; Donald had been vaccinated against polio and Viv's parents are still not certain that the disease was polio. The effects, however, are clear. Donald has been left permanently disabled from the waist down. He is able to walk on crutches, drive, swim, eat, drink and be merry, but he is unable to play sport. Perhaps, for the brother of an England international, that is a blessing in disguise, albeit a mighty perverse one. Instead, Donald has become his brother's fiercest and, since his move to Manchester United, his most attendant critic. Donald, like Viv in his youth, is a United fanatic. He goes to all the home games and, in his broad Nottingham dialect, will give you chapter and verse on who is playing well and who is not. Most often, Viv comes into the latter category. 'He hasn't a clue' is Viv's standard response. But beneath the banter lies mutual respect and, on Donald's side, no outward trace of envy.

Understandably, at the age of four, Viv was too young to remember the horror of the illness or appreciate the enormous strain on the family. All he recollects is the abnormal activity among his aunts and uncles, who by then had also come to live in Nottingham. He remembers more clearly his one and only journey back to his ancestral home eight years later. He didn't like it. 'They lived right out in the sticks, miles away from anywhere and we had to go by bus from Kingston to get there. The journey was unbelievable. There were people hanging off the bus and people on the roof and the driver only used the horn. If anything had come the other way, that would have been it. We were made very welcome, of course, and I liked being able to play cricket with all my cousins – they were very good at making a ball out of a bit of wood. But my aunt got her handbag with her passport and her money pinched in Kingston and that rather ruined the holiday.'

If there was ever any serious intention on the part of the Andersons to leave England and go back to Jamaica, that homecoming must have ended it. Myrtle Anderson still regards Jamaica as her home; for Viv, it was fun, new, different, all sorts of things, but it wasn't home. Home was Nottingham, the castle, buses where you all sat down, and football. Even by that time, there was no doubt in Viv's mind that he was going to be a professional footballer. Equally there was nothing to suggest that he was going to be one, apart from an incident at Bridlington when an old man watched Viv play football on the sands and told his mother that he would be an international one day, which was rather circumstantial evidence. He had talent certainly, but talent, as his mother informed him over and over, did not necessarily lead to success.

His school certainly felt he had talent. He went straight into the first team at Fairham Comprehensive and by the age of fifteen was playing for the city and the county at schoolboy level. That same year he was invited for a trial with Manchester United during the school holidays, the first real sign that football could be more than a hobby. Myrtle Anderson needed rather more convincing, Manchester United or not. Much to his annoyance, she sent Viv back to school for another year with the firm instruction that if he wanted to play football for a living he should have some qualifications behind him. Good advice, as Viv himself now concedes, but wasted on a schoolboy whose bedroom was wall-to-wall Manchester United and whose every dream was Old Trafford. His qualifications turned out to be three CSEs, but that didn't seem important when he was invited back for another trial with Manchester United in the summer of 1972. Towards the end of that summer, the letter of rejection came. It would be interesting to know why the United trainers rejected the tall black kid from Nottingham – too lightweight, too tall for a full-back, no 'bottle'? Whatever the reasons, they cost the club £250,000, the sum they had to pay for the same eleven and a half stone almost fourteen years later.

The rejection was the first real setback Viv had encountered, and the fact that it happened to concern the most important thing in his life made the disappointment all the greater. But his reaction to it was equally important. He cried buckets for ten minutes, blamed his mother for ruining his career by keeping him on at school, and then went out and got a job with a local printer. 'It turned out to be one of the best things that ever happened to me because I got experience of another job for a short time. I was bitterly disappointed at the time, but you can learn as much from failure as from success and I just got on with my life.'

Another trial, with Sheffield United, also ended in failure and that, it seemed, was that until a local scout, Ernie Roberts, spotted Anderson playing in a local league match and asked if he would like a trial rather closer to home.

What, one wonders, took Nottingham Forest so long?

THREE

# LIFE IN THE VILLAGE

Nottingham Forest is a club with bags of history but precious little tradition. While Manchester United are expected to win with style and Arsenal are just expected to win, nothing is expected of Forest. They did win the FA Cup in 1898 and 1959, but, when Brian Clough arrived at the City Ground in 1975, the club's best position in the league had been second in 1967. In contrast, their history is full of firsts: the first club to adopt shinguards (1874), the first club to allow the referee to have a whistle (1878), the first club to play three half-backs (1885) and to have a crossbar instead of tape (1891). Among other distinctions, Forest are also the third oldest club in the Football League, the only one not a limited company and the only one, I should imagine, which began life as a Football and Bandy Club, bandy being a sort of hockey played on ice-covered football pitches.

Not surprisingly perhaps, after a century of non-achievement, the people of Nottingham are not exactly football daft either. As Brian Clough and Charles I have found out to their cost, the East Midlander is not easily impressed. In 1642, at the start of the Civil War, Charles tried to raise his standard at Nottingham but only thirty out of 2000 spectators enlisted for his army so he moved elsewhere. Approximately 340 years later, Clough threatened to do the same if the good people of Nottingham did not come out and support their football team. But even when he banned radio and television coverage of European Cup games, he never entirely succeeded in cajoling the locals out of their armchairs. To start with, they could not entirely believe Forest's success; then when they began to beat the best in Europe they got blasé about it. The truth is that Nottingham, in Lawrie McMenemy's words, is a 'football village', never commanding the morale or allegiance of the town in the way that Liverpool and Everton do on Merseyside and Newcastle and Sunderland do in the north-east.

Nottingham is a strange city. It boasts a very old castle and the oldest pub. It is the home of Boots the chemist and D. H. Lawrence, of Robin Hood, of Larwood and Voce, Torvill and Dean, Forest and County. But there is nothing one can pin down about Nottingham –

no cathedral commanding the skyline, no legendary one-way system, no suspension bridge, just Trent Bridge. Yet it must have some attraction, because people who go there tend to stay. The Anderson family for one, most of the Forest side of the late 1970s for another. O'Neill, Burns, Robertson, Barrett, Lloyd and Birtles have all remained in or near the town, Shilton is only just up the road in Derby and Bowyer moved to Hereford in 1987 after spending all but a few years of his lengthy career with Forest. Even as unsentimental a character as Viv Anderson feels that the attraction of the town is more than just familiarity. He might still be there if Arsenal had not tempted him away in 1984, ten years after his league debut.

'I always joked with the Arsenal players about going back up north. "Can't you smell the air. It's real up here." That sort of thing. But it's obviously more than that. I spent the first twenty-eight years of my life there. All my family and most of my friends are there, so it means a lot to me. Several players who have been born and bred in the city have found it difficult to move away. Garry Birtles was back in Nottingham every available minute after he had been transferred to Manchester United, which was probably why he didn't have such a good time there.'

Anderson jokes that he has run up and down the wings of the City Ground so many times there is now a permanent channel there. But when he first signed apprentice professional forms in November 1972, at the age of sixteen, that sort of regularity seemed as far away as London. At the time, Forest were a First Division side in status, halfway down the Second Division in fact. Under the managership of Matt Gillies, they had been relegated in the 1971–72 season (Derby won the championship under Brian Clough and beat Forest by an aggregate 6–0 that year) and were still relying heavily on the experience of old stagers like Sammy Chapman, John Winfield and Peter Hindley. They seemed to have been playing for Forest since time began and though they were certainly not getting any better, they were strong personalities who dominated the club and, too often, the manager. For a young black full-back hoping to make his way in the game, such men were terrifying.

'I never used to speak to the first-team players when I first went to Forest. Apprentices had to knock on the door of the first-team dressing-room and I was always scared stiff of going in there in case I got stick. I did get stick – often about my colour because I was the only coloured player on the staff – but I don't think it did me any harm.

Now it's very different because the apprentices are always taking the piss out of you, but if I'd done that I'd have been thrown down the toilet or something equally bad. But I think that was the right way because it taught you respect.'

From the safe distance of a decade, Anderson looks back on those days with nostalgia. In retrospect, they were also vital to his career. Throughout his childhood he had been taught to treat his elders as betters but, more importantly, he had been taught to listen. He was selective, mind you. He didn't listen much to his school teachers but he listened to anyone who might be able to tell him something about football. It was going to be his living, after all, and the source of his criticism of today's young apprentices is not that they prick his ego but that they don't listen. 'Instead of being cheeky to the senior players, they should listen to what you have to say about the game. They might learn something. Not that I was any different at their age, thinking I knew it all, but I was prepared to listen.'

That ability to listen had been noticed by Ian Bowyer, one of the first-team players who had been bought by Dave Mackay from Orient for £40,000 in October 1973. Now player/manager of Hereford United in the Fourth Division, Bowyer needed little prompting to recall those early days at Forest. 'You could see even then that Viv had ability. He had a lot of pace and if you've got pace you can get out of trouble much easier. I always thought he was a bit nervous – perhaps that's not quite the right word. But he was respectful, well mannered and had the good sense to listen to older players. That was all down to his upbringing.' Bowyer too was acutely aware of the influence of the older players and of the traditional atmosphere at the club. 'People like Chapman and Winfield had been brought up in a very traditional way. Apprentices and reserve-team players came into the dressing-room, did their jobs and didn't say anything to the older players. There was a strong feeling that everyone knew his place; if you didn't, they were very quick to pick you up about it. That's changed now, reflecting the changes in society. Now kids are a bit cocky, though who's to say which way is right?'

The early discipline of the football club served to reinforce the strict discipline Anderson had been used to at home. He knew his place at home and now he knew his place at work, an important qualification for life under Brian Clough's management. When Clough came, Anderson knuckled under and did as he was told. Others didn't and were never heard of in football again.

Under the stern eyes of Ted, who looked after the apprentices, Anderson had to clean the boots every Friday, and along with the other apprentices clean up the terraces, wash down the dressing-rooms after matches and paint the ground at the start of the season, all the traditional chores that players look back on with a fondness not felt at the time. He had to put up with his fair share of ribbing about his colour from his fellow apprentices, but if it was vicious it either passed Anderson by or he has consciously put it to the back of his mind. Either way, he does not recall it affecting him, though there are different views from two of his contemporaries.

'He didn't seem to be very conscious of his colour early in his career,' said Ian Bowyer. 'It might have been one of the reasons he was so quiet in those days and it was obviously hard for him because he was the only one on the staff. Any stick he got was more from the other apprentices and he was able to handle that because none of them was going any further in the game than he was. Tony Woodcock was a big help to him, but in general we never gave it a second thought. That's how well he coped.'

Martin O'Neill, who came to Forest from Distillery in 1971 with a degree in law and a passion for football, thinks that Anderson became self-conscious about his colour when he began to play for the first team. 'He was very shy and, I think, very aware of his colour. That possibly affected his confidence early on. He was one of the few making an impact on the game in the mid-1970s and that was bound to be difficult, though he laughs it off now. Mark Walters at Rangers and even John Barnes at Liverpool experienced it worse than others because they were the first to play for their particular clubs. And I suppose if I was getting "Irish bastard" thrown at me every five minutes, it would have some affect on me. The players couldn't comprehend it though. To us, he was just another player. In fact, far from there being any prejudice against black players inside the game, I think there was actually considerable sympathy for them. Certainly I would have loved to have been the first manager to have picked a black player, just to show people.'

Anderson never believed that he had to prove himself more than any of the other apprentices to make the grade. And the colour of his skin concerned him as little as the fact that Forest were a club on the way down. This was a professional football club, not a professional football club on hard times, and he wanted to be a professional footballer, black or white. 'I never considered it as the first rung on the ladder to being an England international. It was nothing like that. It's a terrible cliché that footballers take each game as it comes, but in most cases it's true, particularly when you're young. I was about to become a printer, so I was just delighted to be playing football.'

That's not entirely true. Even in those early carefree days, if Anderson did not know what he wanted, characteristically he knew what he didn't want. 'There were two players who were always in the reserves. They were getting on a bit, about twenty-three or twenty-four, and they never seemed to get any further. I remember saying to Tony Woodcock that if I ever became like them I would not stay. They seemed happy being reserves and getting the odd first-team game when someone was injured. I couldn't have stood that.'

There was never much danger that Anderson would languish long in the reserves at Forest, and his promotion was hastened by the arrival of a new manager at the City Ground in the summer of 1973. Dave Mackay knew a good defender when he saw one, and, only a month after he had replaced Matt Gillies, said so in the *Daily Express*: 'The lad who has pleased him (Mackay) most in Forest's pre-season build-up is a 16-year-old coloured defender, Viv Anderson. "I will have no hesitation in naming this lad for a place in the first team as soon as possible," said Mackay.' Though Mackay only stayed a short time at Forest before replacing one Brian Clough up the road at Derby County, Anderson remembers enough about both his attitude and his ability to put him high up the list of the nine managers he has played under. 'He had the reputation of being such a hard man that we didn't quite know what to expect when he arrived, but actually the pre-season training was surprisingly mild and involved a lot of football. I was very impressed by him.' It helps, of course, that a manager thinks you can play, but a sure way to Anderson's heart is through gentle training sessions: lots of football, very little running. Managers are often judged more by their training methods than their playing methods and Mackay had been influenced by the Clough school at Derby. Training was a means to an end, not an end in itself. When he moved to Arsenal, Anderson found out to his horror that not everyone felt that way. Don Howe was a coach; you got better by practising. Clough was not a coach; you got better by playing.

In the youth team, Anderson continued to learn his trade, playing five-a-sides in the courtyard with 3ft-wide goals and practising his block tackles against a wall. The team won a pre-season tournament in Bremen at the start of the 1973–74 season and Anderson was made 'player of the tournament'.

Tony Woodcock remembered him well, though not so much for the standard of his play. 'One evening after a game we were sitting down for a meal and Viv got cramp. He tried to stretch his legs out but his knees were stuck under the table and he couldn't move. We thought it was very funny but, in the end, he just slid under the table screaming and we realised that he wasn't playing around. Then someone suggested that the best way to cure cramp was salt water, so we poured a cupful of salt water down him. He didn't know which was worse, the cramp or the water.'

In his brief stay at Nottingham, Mackay took Forest to the sixth round of the FA Cup and, true to his word, gave Anderson his first-team debut in a pre-season friendly at Walsall. Forest won 2–0 with goals by Duncan McKenzie and Neil Martin, and Anderson played well enough to earn the pithy headline in the local paper: 'Young Viv looks good'. When Mackay replaced Clough at the Baseball Ground in October 1973, the word had obviously been passed on to his successor, Allan Brown, that the 'young coloured defender', as the press continually described him, was worth keeping. On his eighteenth birthday, in 1974, Anderson signed professional forms, and two months later he completed his absurdly untroubled rise to the top by making his league debut, against Sheffield Wednesday at Hillsborough, when Sammy Chapman was in dispute with the club and not available. It was a lucky break, not the last in his career, but Anderson made the most of his short-term opportunity in a 3–2 away win.

This, one might have presumed, would have been a momentous occasion in a young professional's life, etched indelibly in the memory. 'I can remember nothing about the game at all,' said Anderson, a lapse not solely due to football's 'take each game as it comes' mentality. Ask a cricketer about his first-class debut and you will get date, time, weather, scores and emotional nuances. Ask a footballer and you might, if lucky, get the opposition and the score (unless it was 0–4). Football is not a game which encourages reflection or sentiment: there are too many games and to remember one is like trying to recall one brushstroke in a painting. To the ground, change, play, change, away. That's the footballer's rhythm – forty-two times a season. Very rarely will you catch an away team still at the ground more than half an hour after the final whistle, particularly not Forest who are the quick change artistes of the Football League. Anderson recalls the second leg of the European Cup match in 1978 against Liverpool as typical. 'We didn't arrive at the ground until forty minutes before kick-off because Clough reckoned we would miss all the traffic if we went late. We played, held them to a 0–0 draw, and half an hour after the match had finished we were back off to Nottingham.'

Surprisingly, therefore, Anderson does have some idea about his second game in the first team, a League Cup tie against Newcastle at St James's Park. 'Newcastle were a fearsome side then with MacDonald and Tudor and, to be honest, before the match I was terrified. I went to look at the pitch with the rest of the Forest players and only got as far as the end of the tunnel. I poked my nose out, took one look and then went back to the dressing-room. But, when I started playing, it was fine.' Despite being dumped into the hoardings by MacDonald's elbow, Anderson again acquitted himself capably for an 18-year-old. Two more games followed before Sammy Chapman returned and he resumed his career in the reserves.

If you were to chart Anderson's career to this point, the end of 1974, it would be in a steady upward curve. Apprentice, professional, reserves, first team, England youth trials – the graph was becoming increasingly predictable. Only the fact that Forest's fortunes were going in the opposite direction clouded the horizon. Within a week of the start of the New Year, all that had changed. On 3 January 1975, with Forest thirteenth in the Second Division, Allan Brown was replaced. Predictability was out; Clough was in. For Forest and for Anderson, life would never be quite the same.

FOUR

# THE DIRTY DOZEN

'I think it all started within these four walls,' said Martin O'Neill, looking around the inside of a little cafe just round the corner from the City Ground in Nottingham. 'Frank Clarke would come here and tell us stories about his days at Newcastle. All the younger players would come – myself, Viv, Woody, John Robertson – and we would listen open-mouthed because we wanted to do well too. Suddenly, from three or four coming in, everyone was coming. Results started to go well and everything was happening. We built a great spirit and great friendship among the players. In other clubs, there would always be little cliques of three or four players, but not at Forest – when we went out, we all went out together, twelve or thirteen of us. I mean, I could ring them all up now and ask them for a get-together next Monday and know that without fail most of them would be there, not because we wanted to relive anything but just because we were good mates.'

There is something entirely appropriate about the best team in Europe being nourished in the unpretentious warmth of McKay's cafe; Forest were themselves unpretentious, a bread-and-butter team who got by on the straightforward virtues of hard work and friendship, of being 'good mates', in fact. Ability, solidity, naiveté, simplicity, intelligence, luck – Forest had all of those in the 1977-78 season, but, almost above all, they had extraordinary camaraderie. 'It might sound stupid,' said Anderson, 'but it's very important. We got along off the field and on, and all the wives got on as well. That goes a long long way, especially on a Saturday afternoon when you need some help and there are two or three of your team there. Alex Ferguson talks about it now at Manchester United: it makes you look forward to playing and to wanting to win just that bit more.'

Such camaraderie is not something which can be created to order, but somehow – by luck, judgement, act of God, call it what you will – Clough achieved it out of not very promising material. In the film *The Dirty Dozen* Lee Marvin inherited a bunch of raw recruits and ageing drop-outs and turned them into a crack fighting unit. The same kind of thing happened to Nottingham Forest between January 1975 when they were thirteenth in the Second Division and 22 April 1978 when they won their first league title.

For a start, Forest had their share of misfits: Kenny Burns, Larry Lloyd, even Peter Withe. All were strong characters, none had reputations for being ideal club men. They also had their share of raw recruits: notably, Anderson and Woodcock. They were led by a man whose idea of discipline was to make a man play for forty-five minutes with a suspected broken foot and whose idea of punishment was to send his entire first-team squad, internationals and all, running bare-legged through a field of nettles. Above all, like the Dirty Dozen, they developed the streetfighting mentality of the perpetual underdog. Nothing was expected of them so they had nothing to lose.

At the start of the 1977-78 season, no one even mentioned Forest in their pre-season predictions. *The Times* football correspondent, for example, suggested that come April there was no reason to believe that the league championship positions at the end of the previous season would be any different, namely Liverpool, Manchester City, Ipswich. As Liverpool had won the title for three of the last five years and finished second in the other two, that was a bit like predicting rain sometime within the next month. Manchester City had an abundance of talent – Peter Barnes, Dennis Tueart, Dave Watson, Mick Channon, Colin Bell – and only lacked a little consistency, while Ipswich, under Bobby Robson, had finished third in two out of the last three years.

Forest, on the other hand, were among the also-rans, even possible relegation candidates. They had just scraped into the top division, courtesy of Bolton Wanderers, and with only one new signing in the close season (Kenny Burns from Birmingham City for £150,000) Forest, said the scribes, lacked pace and class, particularly in midfield where the names of Bowyer, McGovern and O'Neill were hardly likely to strike fear into the hearts of Case, McDermott, Kennedy and Dalglish. No, as the season opened in bright sunshine, there seemed little doubt that Forest would struggle and the status quo would be maintained. And, in two ways, it was. As in 1977, Liverpool won the European Cup; as in 1977, Liverpool scored fifty-seven points in the league. The only difference was that Forest scored seven more, winning the championship with four games still to go and the League Cup in a replay at Old Trafford against Liverpool. In doing so, they became the first side to complete the double of League and League

Cup, the first side since Alf Ramsey's Ipswich in 1961-62 to win the championship in their first season after promotion and only the third newly promoted side to do so since the war (the push-and-run Spurs of 1950-51 were the other team).

It was a remarkable transformation for a club that had won just two cups in 112 years and it might have been regarded as a fluke, one of those strange and romantic upsets that tend to occur in the third round of the FA Cup in places like Rochdale and Wrexham, were it not for two things: first, Clough had done almost exactly the same thing to Derby County a few years previously and second, the success of that 1977-78 season was just the start. Two European Cups, another League Cup and a Super Cup were to find their way into Forest's boardroom in the next three years. Pot-hunting of that order cannot be a fluke.

There was an equally remarkable transformation in the careers of many of the Forest players, none more so than Anderson's. Although on the verge of being moved on, as they say in the trade, during Clough's early days, Anderson was an England international inside two years. Tony Woodcock, who could have been bought by Graham Taylor at Lincoln City for £5000 in 1976, was sold to Cologne for £600,000 in 1980, and John Robertson moved from reserve-team player to Scottish international in a similar time. All of them acknowledge without hesitation their debt to Clough. Like him or loathe him – and there is often a bit of both – he made them.

'Whatever you think about him as a person, in the end, without Clough, I would probably still be a run-of-the-mill Second or Third Division player,' Anderson said. 'Being part of that Forest side and enjoying the success we had gave us all tremendous confidence. I developed as a person and as a footballer under him and I was able to capitalize on that at Arsenal and Manchester United.' If there is a moral in all this, it is that success and failure, the difference between a personalized black Mercedes at Manchester United and a Ford Fiesta cadged off the local garage in Halifax (footballers tend to measure success in such terms) is one backroom decision, a few anonymous games out of position or some extra gate receipts at Lincoln City.

Looking back, Anderson now realizes that Clough's first two years when the playing staff was being assessed and, in general, maimed, were the turning point in his career. The omens for Anderson were not good, for one of Clough's first acts was to drop him for a cup replay at Tottenham. Anderson had played in the first game and had to come off with cramp. Before the replay, Clough took his squad down to Bisham Abbey for a few days' training. Woodcock was taken, Anderson was not. 'I remember thinking at the time: 'That's a good start.' I learnt later that he took the assistant manager John Sheridan into his office and told him to write down a list of players to take to Bisham. Woody went, but when he came back he said he'd only been taken so Cloughie could make fun of him. He spent the whole of the time there running errands for Clough. "Woodcock, get me the sugar." He even had to clean Clough's shoes. He never saw a ball the whole time so he wasn't very impressed, but it certainly made an impact.'

According to Clough, however, he knew about Anderson's talent before he ever came to the City Ground through the recommendation of the same John Sheridan. During his disastrous 44-day spell at Leeds, Clough was about to sell Terry Cooper to Forest and asked Sheridan about any promising youngsters on the Forest staff for a possible part-exchange deal. Sheridan apparently said that Anderson was the best and Clough came to Forest to watch him play sweeper in a reserve game. In the end, the deal fell through and Anderson stayed at the City Ground.

For a few games in that 1974-75 season, Anderson played in midfield. A few more and he could have been on his way to Darlington or somewhere equally prosperous, for by his own admission he was never built to be a midfield player – 'too much like hard work' – and he was lost. Luckily, for him and for Forest, the new manager could see it too and he was returned to his rightful position at full-back. In Clough's first full season at the club (without Peter Taylor, who had stayed on at Brighton when Clough moved to Leeds), Forest finished eighth and Anderson was in and out of the side, playing in half of the league games. In the close season, Taylor joined Clough at Forest with orders to sort out the playing side. Taylor's response, recorded in his book *With Clough*, was typically forthright. 'They're nice lads and no trouble,' he told Clough after seeing Forest play in two pre-season friendlies. 'But that was a feat by you to finish eighth in the Second Division because some of them are only Third Division players . . .' Anderson himself does not know if that description fitted him at the time. Probably not, because in the following season he played almost every game. Yet, when Anderson received his first England cap, Taylor recalled how close he had come to signing another right-back. 'His biggest problem when I first came to the club was that he did not walk tall. I had to get him to believe in himself and I smashed him verbally. But Viv is not the sort of person to have a go back at you. He's one of the quietest lads in the game. He got the message pretty quickly, though, and as I told him at the time we were not willing to wait long for him to reveal the skill we knew he possessed. I told him we had a right-back lined up, and it wasn't just management talk to get the best out of him; we were ready to buy someone. But he ruled out the possibility with his performances for us.'

Bravado? Arrogance? Taking credit where it isn't due? A little of all three perhaps, but Anderson himself remembers one incident which backs up the theory that for a time his career at Forest hung by a thread. 'Clough dropped me once early on and when I asked why, he said: "Because you're too quiet." Looking back on it, that could have finished me off. I was only young and a criticism like that is pretty hard to take, because that's your character. It's hard for people to believe now, because quietness is not one of my characteristics, but at that time I was very quiet. He was right, of course. You can't play football in silence. I don't think I changed my character overnight, but it certainly made me think and I consciously tried to come out of myself a little more.'

The nervousness that Anderson obviously felt in the company of the new manager was not confined to him. Ian Bowyer, recently signed from Orient, was also wondering what was in store. 'When Brian came to Forest and brought Jimmy Gordon with him as trainer, there was a nervous twelve months when no one was quite sure how to treat him. Everybody was a little on edge because Clough had a reputation from his Derby days and from being sacked by Leeds. He was weighing everyone up and likewise we were trying to get to know him. Certainly there were a few comings and goings at that time and Viv was in and out of the team. It was an interesting time, but it did us no harm. I think Viv was made to think about the game more and that was true of all of us. We were all being told to look at our game more carefully, at what we were trying to do and why and being asked to improve one or two per cent. Viv was no different. He was an ambitious young man and he wanted to do well. Very soon we were starting to get the taste of success and Viv wanted to be a part of that.'

In one of those strange quirks of fate that almost every professional sportsman can point to in a successful career, a severe leg injury at the end of the 1975-76 season, which threatened to end Anderson's career almost before it had begun, in fact proved decisive. For the first time since he had been rejected by Manchester United and for absolutely the first time in his professional career, Anderson came face to face with adversity. And out of the confrontation emerged a more determined professional. Anderson said: 'I can remember the incident as clearly as yesterday. This lad called Lindsay caught me across the left knee. I stood up and my knee was completely out of place, so I pushed it back into position and lay down again. The doctor couldn't believe it.' Luckily for Anderson, the injury came right at the end of the season and he had three months to recover. It was a testing time for his character and his patience, but he worked hard through the summer, impressed Clough with his dedication and was rewarded with a regular place in the first team six weeks into the new season. As Clough remarked when selecting him for his first game back after injury, 'He has made a staggering return after what was a serious injury and this is reward for the effort he has put into his comeback. What he must now do is convince himself that he is good enough to stay in the side. He has been a little more positive in his attitude, but he has to think positively as well.' Adversity can concentrate the mind wonderfully and the sudden realization that life was not all one long freewheel downhill must have come as a shock to a boy who had not had to think too hard about his profession up to then. From that day to this, Anderson has done extra weight-training on that left leg to strengthen the knee ligaments. It has provided a daily reminder that a footballer's life is as up-and-down as a steeplejack's and just as precarious.

Anderson's performances after his return in October 1976 ended the uncertainty about Forest's right-back spot for the next ten years. In his first match back, against Sheffield United, he scored his first goal for the club and, according to reliable sources, did a lap of honour, blowing kisses to the crowd in a Caribbean-style display of exuberance. They thrashed United 6–1, prompting one scribe to write prophetically: 'Here was an attacking display of the highest class and an all-round sense of purpose and confidence which reminded me forcibly of Derby's promotion season in 1969.'

Derby, however, entered the First Division with rather more style than Forest. They gained promotion by seven points from Crystal Palace while Forest looked out of the race until they won four of their last five games. Even then they had to wait while Bolton tried to get five out of the last six points, only failing in the final match of the season at home against Wolves. Typically, Forest were sunning themselves in the Majorcan sunshine as Bolton lost. From the side Clough inherited when he arrived at the club, only four played in the final match of the season against Millwall: John Middleton, the goalkeeper, Ian Bowyer, Martin O'Neill and Sammy Chapman. Three others – Anderson, Woodcock and Robertson – had been playing for the reserves; the rest had been bought for a song.

Before the start of the following year, the only newcomer was Kenny Burns, a centre-forward who had scored nineteen goals for Birmingham City the previous season. Clough had paid £150,000 for him and then played him at centre-back in place of Sammy Chapman. Apart from Peter Shilton and, later, Archie Gemmill, the jigsaw was complete, a fact that football didn't notice – until too late.

A furrow slowly crossed the brow of the football world during that epic 1977-78 season. Journalists are not the quickest people in the world to admit that they are wrong and it took until Christmas for them grudgingly to entertain the notion that Forest were at the top of the table to stay. No one could really believe it as some reports of Forest's matches will testify:

*20 August: Everton 1 Nottingham Forest 3.*
'Forest's victory at Goodison Park was the finest, most surprising result of the day. Keeping true to his new-found modesty, manager Brian Clough commented: "We played reasonably well".'

*23 August: Nottingham Forest 1 Bristol City 0*
'Forest may not have the players to reach the peaks of the First Division but their attractive and intelligent football will give a great deal of pleasure.'

*30 August (League Cup, second round): Nottingham Forest 5 West Ham 0*
'It is not often in the modern game that a full-back is exposed in the way Lampard was by Robertson. With Robertson on the left and O'Neill wide on the right, breaking from midfield, Forest are a practical and attractive team.'

*3 September: Arsenal 3 Nottingham Forest 0*
'Brian Clough has always been something of an illusionist. But not even his sleight of hand could disguise the fact that his side scarcely looked championship material . . . Perhaps deep down the provincials were overawed by the marble halls of north London.'

*17 September: Nottingham Forest 2 Villa 0*
'The most surprising thing is the way players who have been around awhile are having a new lease of life, playing with more enthusiasm and determination.'

*4 October: Nottingham Forest 4 Ipswich 0* (Forest go back to the top, there to remain until the end of the season.)

*15 October: Nottingham Forest 2 Manchester City 1*
'Where is this all going to end? A team of basically ordinary souls with an almost excessive belief in themselves and the good sense of knowing their strengths and playing to them.'

*12 November: Nottingham Forest 2 Manchester United 1*
'Forest are a team devoid of celebrities; a mixture of fresh and well-worn faces who ought to be slogging it out at the bottom of the table.'

*26 November: West Bromwich Albion 0 Nottingham Forest 0* (Forest start a run of forty-two unbeaten league games, which stretches into the middle of the following season.)

*17 December: Manchester United 0 Nottingham Forest 4*
'Robertson and O'Neill gave United a roasting along the flanks. Forest are equipped to win the Championship.'

*8 February (League Cup semi-final, first leg): Leeds 1 Nottingham Forest 3*
'Forest played beautifully simple football, like an innocently perceptive child's painting.'

*22 February (Leage Cup semi-final, second leg): Nottingham Forest 4 Leeds 2*
'The secret of Forest's success is teamwork. Each man plays for his fellows; they have peace, spirit and vision of a wide field.'

Not before time, as Forest rolled on, the accolades began to roll in, not all of them as eloquent or as accurate as that last one by Geoffrey Green in *The Times*. The press had, not surprisingly, misread Forest, but when it came down to it so too had the Forest players. Though they felt confident that they would survive where most thought they would not, their confidence did not stretch much further; none of the players' contracts had included a bonus for winning the League. That sort of omission would be unheard of now, but it sums up the players' naiveté as well as their lack of expectation.

Peter Taylor, Forest's ever-confident assistant manager, said before the start of the season that he would be pleased if the team managed to get into Europe. His ebullience did not encompass the League. But Peter Shilton's did. Shilton came to Forest from Stoke a month after the start of the season and he thought then that the team had something others had overlooked.

'I watched Forest play Wolves on television early in the season. I was up for sale because Stoke had just been relegated and I knew that Cloughie wanted to buy me. Watching Forest then, I honestly thought that, if I could join them, they would do really well. They were 66–1 for the title at the time and when I knew I was going to Forest I wanted to put a bet on. But I didn't in the end and have been kicking myself ever since,' said Shilton.

By general consent, Shilton's arrival was vital to Forest's success. Not that his predecessor, John Middleton, had done anything wrong; even Clough said as much. Most managers would have been happy with having the England Under-21 goalkeeper in their side, but then most managers aren't Clough. Clough reckons to make ten decisions a week. If seven are right and three are wrong, then he still feels he's made more right decisions than most managers. Management, he says, is all about taking decisions. So Middleton went to Derby and Shilton, after a wrangle over a loyalty bonus, moved to Forest.

The impact he made was immediate. Having conceded five goals in their previous two games, Forest let in just one in the next five league games, and only twenty-four in the whole season. But it was not just his goalkeeping that made an impression on Anderson.

'His name went before him and as a young player I was a bit nervous about him because I valued his opinion and I didn't want to let him down. That made me concentrate just that little bit harder. He has a high opinion of his own ability, which gives you confidence too, and he's a very hard taskmaster. He's always shouting at you, sometimes a bollocking for something, often encouragement. That's good: quiet goalkeepers are nightmares – except Pat Jennings, who was brilliant. But, in the end, having Shilton simply meant extra points in the bag. I remember in particular one save he made at Coventry that season. It was 0–0 when he stopped a shot from Ferguson from about six yards and so we got the point which won us the league. Pete was the best shot-stopper I've played with. Pat Jennings maybe commanded his area better and was better on crosses but for reflex saves I would choose Peter. Peter always wanted to do things by the book, but Pat would stop the ball with anything – arms, legs, shoulder, the lot. I've been lucky to play in front of those two.'

The statistics show Shilton's contribution to the team. Forest's defence – Shilton, Anderson, Lloyd, Burns and Frank Clarke or Colin Barrett – was the best in the league. The figures give other pointers to Forest's success that season. For a start, they used just sixteen players throughout the season and at one period in the New Year, when injuries are starting to hit most teams hard, they went nine games with an unchanged side. Whether that was because they did very little training – rather like Liverpool who are traditionally less prone to injury than other teams – or just sheer luck is hard to tell. But consistency of personnel, as any manager, industrial or football, will tell you, is vital for success. Newcastle, for example, used thirty-five players in the same season and were relegated.

In contrast, Forest were not prolific goalscorers nor did they have one prolific goalscorer. They scored sixty-nine goals, a total bettered by both Everton and Manchester City, who finished third and fourth, and their two top scorers, Withe and Robertson, with twelve each, together were still six short of Latchford's thirty goals for Everton. But the difference with Forest was that everyone scored – Woodcock (eleven), O'Neill (eight), Bowyer, Burns, McGovern, Needham (four), even Anderson managed three – and, above all, everyone scored at home and away. Remarkably, Forest only scored five more goals at home than away. 'I have long since discovered the fact that it's no good scoring goals at one end if you are letting them in at the other,' as Clough once said. Solid defence, quick breaks, simplicity: those are the hallmarks of his teams.

Ask any member of the team to reveal the secret of Forest's success and they will look at you with a face half puzzled by the meaning of the question, half sympathetic at the innocence of it, and reply: 'We just went out and played.' The temptation is to add a 'Brian' on the end. But, in this case, it is not lack of analysis that produces a deadpan answer like that, it's truth. Clough's teams are not bogged down by theory, systems, dossiers and all the tactical claptrap that delights journalists and confuses players. They *do* just go out and play. But they play to their strengths and, above all, their limitations. They didn't have anybody who could hit a sixpence with a forty-yard pass, so they didn't play forty-yard passes; they didn't have great pace, so they played to feet not into space. When they had the ball, they tried to keep it; when they didn't, they bullied the opposition into giving it back: all the basic principles of football that sports masters up and down the country have been drumming into earnest pupils for years.

Just go out and play. Simple, if you have good players. And, at that time, Forest had two of the best. Shilton was well known and expensive. John Robertson was unheard of and, when he arrived as a forlorn apprentice from his native Scotland in the early 1970s, very cheap.

When Clough and Taylor joined forces at Forest in the summer of 1976, Robertson was trying to play in the centre of midfield for the reserves. He was, according to Taylor, overweight, sloppy in dress and habit, and hovering on the brink of failure as a professional footballer. Two years later, by common consent, he was the key player in the most successful side in Britain.

'John always had ability,' said Anderson. 'I can remember when we were both in the reserve team, we would play five-a-side in this small courtyard. One game, John nutmegged me about fifty times. Usually you would say that was a fluke, but he did it so often it must have been more than that. It taught me a lesson because I very rarely get nutmegged these days, but it showed what tremendous ability he had. He was lazy and he had always been podgy because, as Clough and Taylor kept on reminding everyone, he liked his chips. He was quicker than you would think over ten yards, but not lightning like Franz Carr, and he was very hard to knock off the ball because he was so heavily built.

'In his early days at Forest, he wanted to play in the centre of midfield but Clough or Taylor converted him to play on the left wing. It wasn't that they found something new in him, they just played him in the right place. He was a unique player. I mean, there aren't many fat and slow left-wingers around.'

Fat and slow, perhaps, but the tubby little Scot was blessed with that priceless asset, a footballing brain. He knew what was 'off', in football lingo. 'He knew what he was doing the whole time,' recalled Anderson. 'He knew when to take people on, when not to, when to hold it, when to cross it, when not to cross it. It made my job a lot easier. When Robbo got the ball I'd start winding up down the right just in advance of the centre-halves so that I was ready to attack and cover, if necessary. But I could rely on him not giving the ball away so I could go forward knowing that I would probably not get caught.'

Of course, the truth is that Robertson wasn't a real winger at all. Wingers are fast, tricky, temperamental, selfish. They play a game all of their own and never do what they should. Robertson was not like that. Unlike card-carrying wingers, he didn't find it an irresistible personal challenge to round all three of the opponents queueing up to tackle him. He simply laid the ball back inside to one of the other midfield players, thereby effectively playing three opponents out of the game. He was lazy enough to take the easy option. For the first part of the 1977-78 season, few sides bothered to put more than one on him, which was equally fatal. He only needed half a yard to right or left of the full-back to centre the ball, either in a slow tantalizing parabola to the far post or with vicious swing to the near. It didn't take long for other teams to discover that there was a certain consistency to the Forest pattern. It took rather longer for them to find out what to do about it.

'We were very much a left-sided team,' explained Martin O'Neill. 'Woodcock always turned left, Withe invariably went left, Gemmill shovelled things left. Most moves went through Robbo because he was absolutely brilliant. He had so many strings to his bow it didn't really matter what the opposition did. He could go either way and only needed half a yard to whip a cross in or he could play a precise twenty-yard ball in to the feet of the centre-forward without having to beat a man. As long as he was given the ball without being closed down too quickly, he was OK. Even if he was, he could just shovel the ball back to the full-back and wait for another opportunity.

'It must have been hell for the opposition full-backs because John would pick the ball up deep, amble – that's probably the best word to use – up the pitch and then he would play a twenty-yard ball into Woodcock or Withe on the edge of the box, who could turn and get a cross in. The full-back is looking at Robbo and thinking, "Well, that's my job done"; and all the action is going on behind him. Now his manager is telling him to get back round and challenge Woodcock. So he's completely confused because he's not quite sure what his job is. He goes back to challenge, so Woodcock just lays the ball back to Robertson thirty yards further up the field. Dead simple, but then that's football.'

With his Irish gift of the gab and his degree in law, O'Neill is an unusual and amusing footballing character. He came to Forest from Distillery in 1971 and was one of the few to survive the early Clough regime. He is not one to keep silent about what he feels is injustice and so his relationship with the autocratic Forest manager was not often an easy one. 'I was always in and out of the manager's office. I once used the word 'victimize' and he threw me out. I wanted to play central midfield where I would have more of a chance to dribble and go at defences, but, in the end, I would have played anywhere because I was desperate to be part of a winning team.' After spells with Norwich, Manchester City and Notts County, O'Neill had to retire from the game early because his knees would no longer take the strain. Only half jokingly, he attributes the extra wear and tear to covering for Anderson in those early days.

O'Neill said: 'It was Viv's job to defend – under any Brian Clough team, defenders are supposed to defend first and foremost – but he was better going forward than defending. That's not to say he couldn't defend because he could – in five-a-side games he was generally first pick because he was so difficult to get past – but most defenders don't like being taken on one-to-one and Viv wouldn't deny the fact that with his pace and long stride he looked better going forward. I remember Rix of Arsenal saying: 'Give me a chance to get at him.' But because I was generally covering in front of him doing the same job as Coppell at Manchester United and Case at Liverpool, he very rarely had to make a tackle. Had he had a less strong player than me he would have found it much harder. In all honesty, he was very lucky to have me there.'

While perhaps not giving him the size of byline O'Neill would have liked, Anderson did appreciate the efforts of the tough little Irishman. 'He had a frightening amount of ability and was very strong on the ball. When we played "keep ball" sessions in training, Martin had a ball all to himself, no one could ever get it off him. He was always an outlet for me on the right touchline and we worked up and down the right side together. He got more than his fair share of goals, but I don't think the management really appreciated what a good player he was until he left and they tried to replace him. He worked very hard helping me and other people.' O'Neill would greet such sentiments with a hearty 'hear, hear'. He never felt appreciated and now says that he actually thought he played the best football of his career when he was given a less restricted role under John Bond at Norwich, which just goes to show that not even Clough can get the best out of all his players all of the time.

If O'Neill and Bowyer both thought that Robertson was the key player in that championship season, Anderson points to the combination of Burns and Lloyd at the centre of Forest's impregnable defence as being the decisive factor. The defender's view? Perhaps, but Burns, the backstreet kid from Glasgow, strong, robust and, in Anderson's words, 'as hard as nails', and Lloyd, big-headed, temperamental a man who once aimed a punch at Anderson on the field and who threatened to do the same to Peter Taylor at a team meeting, were an awesome combination. 'It was just their sheer physical presence,' said Anderson. 'Frightened is not the right word to use, it was just that other teams didn't look forward to playing against them because of their reputation. You'd be surprised how important a part that plays in the game. Some people thrive on the physical challenge, but 90 per cent don't like to know they are going to be in for a hard time. I mean, if you know every time you hang on to the ball you will get hammered, you get rid of it quicker than you might do with other defenders.' Bowyer confirmed, 'Kenny knew people didn't like playing against him and he'd play on that to the extent that he would threaten to volley them out if they ever came in our penalty-box. You could see teams would come to our place and Larry would sort one out and Kenny would sort the other out – fairly and squarely for the most part, though with Burnsy there as a very thin line between fair and unfair. But after ten minutes their strikers would be looking over their shoulders and thinking: "There's nothing for us here." I believe that first season was Burns's best year. He was made Footballer of the Year by the football writers. Can you believe it? A rogue like Burns alongside gentlemen of the game like Sir Stanley Matthews and Tom Finney. It's unbelievable.'

Unbelievable or not, Forest began the season winning and just kept on doing so. They were lucky with their fixtures; they played Everton, who for much of the season were their main rivals for the championship, on the opening day of the season when muscles are still being stretched and results can go a bit haywire, and they played Liverpool on the last day, when it didn't matter any more. They were even lucky to catch Liverpool on a rare off-season (though they did win the European Cup) when the loss of three successive league games in November caused the word 'crisis' to be whispered down the corridors of Anfield. Bob Paisley responded by purchasing Graeme Souness from Middlesbrough, a move which most probably denied Forest their second championship in the following season.

While their rivals lacked consistency, Forest ploughed on. They had a momentary hiccough against Arsenal on their first visit to London when, for the first and last time, Burns stepped out of line and was fined, and lost two out of three games early in November. But, after their victory against Ipswich on 4 October, Peter Withe scoring all four goals in a 4–0 victory, Forest went top of the table and stayed there until the following May. The second of those two defeats heralded the extraordinary unbeaten run of forty-two league games which stretched into the middle of the following season.

Anderson, young, impressionable and desperate for success, was so caught up in the routine of winning that one victory simple merged into another. 'We just got into a rhythm – train, play, win or draw, train, play, win or draw. The older players kept saying, "Enjoy this because it doesn't come that often," but for me and Woody and the younger players this was all we had known, so we didn't really appreciate our success at the time. Only now when we are really striving hard to win something for Manchester United, who haven't won a title in twenty-one years, do I fully understand what they were saying.'

The fact that the First Division and winning was a relatively novel experience to most of the players was a huge strength, even to older players like Ian Bowyer. 'We didn't know what it was like to go to Old Trafford and Anfield. We went there for the most part fresh and innocent and played with an almost cavalier approach and a far higher level of freedom than in later years. When we started to play in Europe, we had to be more cautious so when we came back to the league we found it hard to readjust. But that season was very very exciting.'

It is hard for professional footballers to pick out individual games from a season ten years ago, even from the most memorable season of their careers. But one game has not been sifted through the memory. On 17 December, Forest went to Old Trafford. In one sense, it was not a big game. United, under Dave Sexton, were not challenging for the title. In fact, just the opposite; they were fourteenth. But such is the extraordinary tradition of footballing excellence at Old Trafford that even Forest knew that if they were serious about winning the title, they had to show it to the world at Old Trafford. 'If we are going to do it, this is the place,' as one of the senior players intoned before the game. Forest did do it, of course. United's wingers, Hill and Coppell, missed two good opportunities in the first fifteen minutes, Brian Greenhoff put through his own net and that effectively was the last United saw of the game, Woodcock scoring two and Robertson one as Forest won 4–0.

'I remember coming off the pitch with Tony Woodcock and just stopping to look around and take it all in. We had murdered them and it was a great feeling. Though I didn't realize it at the time, I think that was a very crucial game, the moment when we really did believe we were good enough to win the League,' said Anderson. Equally important, the following day Forest flew out to Benidorm for a mid-winter break, which took them away from the post-match media hype. They returned for a four-game Christmas programme fresher than ever. Home draws against an out-of-sorts Liverpool, and nearest challengers Everton, plus run-of-the-mill wins against Newcastle and Bristol City gave them six out of eight points, confirming the impression they had given at Old Trafford that they could, and most probably would, be champions. They were helped by other results. Everton lost twice in three days, 6–2 to Manchester United and 3–1 to Leeds. By the New Year, Forest were even-money favourites to win the title.

The only danger for Forest as the long run-in started was fatigue, that weariness of mind and limb that the league system in England refuses to recognize. While most European clubs were enjoying a month off in the middle of the season, Forest were slogging it out through snow, rain and mud on three fronts. It's football's Somme mentality. Nothing should be won easily. Above all, no one should be allowed to win more than their share of the prizes. So, like weightlifters being given heavier and heavier weights to lift until finally their spirit and their strength are crushed, Forest played twenty-four games in just over twelve weeks, including one spell of six in thirteen days. Yet, despite – perhaps even because of – that burden, Forest flourished. If their progress to the championship was more of a steady tramp, their path to the League Cup final was, metaphorically at least, strewn with flowers and littered with dejected refugees: West Ham 5–0, Notts Co. 4–0, Aston Villa 4–2, Bury 3–0 and, most satisfying of all for Clough, whose fourty-four days at Elland Road will not qualify as the happiest of his life, an aggregate 7–3 against Leeds in the semi-final. At the end of the trail of destruction, as one journalist put it, lay Armageddon, a meeting of immovable object and irresistible force, a League Cup final against Liverpool at Wembley.

Forest were comprehensively outplayed at Wembley, but survived and won the replay at Old Trafford with a disputed penalty. Though they did not realize the significance of it at the time, the manner of the victory was as important as the result. Forest had matched Liverpool over two games, had absorbed their pressure and come out on top. When the draw for the European Cup paired them together, that must have given Forest great heart.

After the disappointment of being knocked out of the FA Cup in the fifth round 2–0 by West Bromwich Albion, Forest turned their full concentration back to the league. Everton and Manchester City had both, at one time or another, crept to within two points of the leaders but only because they had played three more games than Forest. In April, Forest played eight league matches, and in the sixth of them, an undistinguished goalless draw at Coventry, won their first title in 112 years. 'We were very lucky even to get a point,' said Anderson. 'We didn't play particularly well, but Peter Shilton pulled off a fantastic point-blank save from Ferguson a few minutes from time and that won us the championship. After the match, we were all too tired to celebrate very much.'

From a personal point of view, there were other things for Anderson to celebrate. Early in March 1978 he was selected for his country for the first time in a quarter-final of the Under-21 European championship. England won 2–1, with two goals by Tony Woodcock, at Maine Road, launching an international career which just eight months earlier had seemed marginally more improbable than Forest doing the double. Somewhere along the line, Anderson turned from an 'also-ran' (Brian Clough's word, not mine) into an England international of the future. Anderson cannot tell you when, but Peter Shilton noticed the change.

'When I first arrived at Forest, Viv hadn't been in the first team that long and he hadn't played in the First Division before. He was quite immature and had a little bit of an inferiority complex about his colour. The management used to have a dig about it and I think that was good because it brought it out into the open and he started to become much more confident. Whether it was just in that season or over several seasons, I don't know, but he blossomed from being a naive person into a mature international. I think it is fair to say that in the early days, if he hadn't have been at such a good club with such forceful management and such a good team, he might not have overcome that little bit of shyness nor found his confidence. Who knows?'

FIVE

# CLOUGH

Unique, unpredictable, brilliant, impossible, impenetrable, unbelievable, mad: at one time or another during the course of our conversations, Anderson used all those adjectives to describe Brian Clough. 'What was it like to play for Clough?' is still the question he gets asked the most, by public and players, which bearing in mind he left Forest in 1984 is a tribute to the staying power of the Clough legend. Anderson's answer is well rehearsed: 'He's a top-class manager and I have enormous respect for him, but he's not someone I'd go drinking with.'

A lot of our talk revolved around Clough. It wasn't planned that way; it was just that his name kept creeping up on us quite unexpectedly, like a recurring episode in a dream. I have the suspicion that Anderson is still frightened of Clough and once suggested as much. At the time we were talking about Clough's methods of management and about how much fear was part of them.

'It can't be fear for everyone – not for experienced professionals like Larry Lloyd and John O'Hare, surely. It was a question of wanting to do well, to play in a successful side, I don't know. I mean, if I went back to Forest now, he wouldn't rule me by fear, would he?'

'I think he might, yes,' I replied. Pause.

'I'd want to do well for the manager, whoever he was.'

'But you'd want to do extra well for Clough because you'd be frightened of his reaction?' Pause.

'Yes, perhaps,' said Anderson hesitatingly, 'because I respect him so much.'

Well, it was an admission of a sort, but on reflection not a surprising one, as Ian Bowyer pointed out. 'When Cloughie arrived at Forest, Viv was still very much a boy and he would never have come across anyone like Clough in his life. Clough, of course, knew that and he played on it. He would generally pick on the younger players because they wouldn't want to jeopardize their place in the team, particularly when we were winning so much. He had a very sharp tongue, accusing players of having a heart the size of a pea, for example, but you can take a lot if you're winning. Viv grew up, of course, and learned to stand up for himself a bit more, but that sort of early influence is hard to lose.'

One incident early in Anderson's Forest days illustrates Clough's selective use of fear to establish his dominance over the players. Just a few hours before the start of a new season the Forest players had still refused to sign their bonus sheets for the season because they were dissatisfied with the terms. The team had agreed to take a collective stand on the issue. With about an hour to go before kick-off, Clough came into the dressing-room and asked about the bonus sheets.

'We're not signing them,' said one of the older players.

'You and you, sign those bonus sheets. You're lucky to be in this team,' replied Clough pointing to Anderson and John Middleton, the two youngest.

They signed. Next he told the club captain, John McGovern, to sign too. He did, followed by the rest of the team.

'I'd have signed anything,' recalled Anderson. 'I wanted to be a part of the team and, of course, Cloughie knew that.'

Fear or knowing which side your bread is buttered, there is a thin dividing line between the two. Clough's autocratic methods only work if they are backed up by success and by players who are hungry for success. At Leeds, they didn't work. The Leeds players had been successful under another manager and didn't need Clough's posturing. So the basis of his authority was undermined and he was forced to resign after forty-four days. In later years, when he was manager of Bolton, John McGovern, quiet, studious and a Clough favourite (Clough brought him to all the clubs he managed) reputedly tried out a Clough-type attack on Peter Reid. McGovern told Reid that he looked scruffy and should go and get shaved. Reid, an experienced pro but not at that time an England international, refused. What does a manager do then? Fine him? Suspend him? Clough would have done, if necessary, but he rarely had to because the player knew that if he stepped out of line he would be off to another – less successful – club. Clough did once tell Garry Birtles to get shaved. Birtles protested that he preferred to play unshaven and then did what he was told. But that was on the bus just before a European Cup final when only two years earlier Birtles had been a carpet-layer and playing for Long Eaton. Professionals will swallow mouthfuls of their pride to be successful and for four years at Forest there was no more successful club in Europe. McGovern did not last long in management.

'You can't compare Clough with any other manager,' Anderson recalled. 'It's not fair to try. I remember one morning at training, it was a really cold day and we all had tracksuit bottoms on. Clough comes along and says: "Right, tracksuit bottoms off, run in and out of there," pointing to a field of nettles next to the training ground.' Consciously enhancing the legend? All part of maintaining his dominance? A power craze or inspired leadership? No one – not even John McGovern, who was with Clough throughout his long career – can tell you what drives Clough. Perhaps he was just in a bad mood that day. 'We were stung to high heaven, but we all went – Shilton, Burns, Lloyd, Francis, all experienced internationals. So I wasn't going to argue about it. In fact, we all had to go through again. It was the law of the playground, but it worked because nobody argued back. Even now, ten years on, I'd probably do the same.

'Clough's whole philosophy is geared to winning, his methods, his discipline, even his bonuses. For example, he'd say: "How many points won the League last year?" and the answer, say, was sixty. He'd say: "Well, you don't get any bonuses until you've got over fifty points," and then he'd give us something silly like £1000 a point. That was before the 1978–79 season and we did quite well out of it because we got sixty points. But I was with him nearly ten years at Forest, and I still hadn't any idea what he was going to do next or what sort of a person he really is by the time I left.'

Abuse, collective and personal, was very much the order of the day in the Forest dressing-room at that time. Anderson, as one of the younger players still learning his trade, came in for more than most. 'I used to get slaughtered every week and that was right because I was probably making more mistakes than some of the others. I was still learning the game, but, whatever he said, I used to be in the team every week and that was all that mattered. Some managers wouldn't dare upset some of the older players, but Clough (Anderson never calls him by his first name) would go for the jugular, if he felt it was justified, whoever it was. He would have a go at John Robertson for being a tramp, for being overweight, but he and Peter Taylor turned him into the best winger in the country. He used to call Larry Lloyd "big head". Now Larry's about 7 foot 6 and Clough's only about 5 foot 10. It wouldn't bother him. It's a very thin dividing line between an insult and a joke. But he was the boss and that was it. Everyone was tarred with the same brush.

'It was not that players didn't argue. Lloyd always wanted to speak up. But Clough always had to have the last word. You'd never get the better of him; he has a very sharp tongue – some of the things he said to Justin Fashanu when he came were very spiteful – and he would have to be right. So after a while nobody bothered arguing because we knew we would get home earlier if we didn't.'

If Clough deliberately cultivated this air of unpredictability, it worked. As John Rowlinson and John Motson remarked in their book on the European Cup, Clough could be 'polite and considerate one minute, brusque and obnoxious the next. This penchant for keeping those around him guessing was one reason why his players were always nicely on edge, never likely to give anything below their best.'

Having been beaten, the players would come into the dressing-room fearing the worst and be given three days off, backed up by a fine if any of them were seen inside the ground before the allotted time. After a good win, when they were all feeling pleased with themselves, they would be mercilessly torn apart. Criticism was common currency, praise a rare, and therefore much sought-after, commodity. 'If he said I had a good game, I would be walking around ten feet tall for the whole weekend,' as Tony Woodcock recalled.

The key to the Clough philosophy, in Anderson's view, is those precious ninety minutes on a Saturday afternoon. For Clough and for all his players, that was the time that you earned your money, you earned your respect and you earned your points. Everything – discipline, training, mental preparation, relaxation, running through nettles, the unpredictability – was geared to getting the best out of eleven individuals for a tiny percentage of the week. But the difference between Clough and about 90 per cent of managers is that he regarded that as a mental test, not a physical one. He was never very interested in training. The Wolves coach, Sammy Chung, once boasted that he could make the fittest member of the Forest side physically sick within three minutes. 'When they give points for that, I'll give you a call,' replied Clough. After the players had reached a certain level of fitness, training was to keep the players occupied, interested and relaxed during the week. Nothing more. Forest never worked on set pieces, never spent their time planning how to counteract other teams' set-piece play. They went for walks down by the Trent, often took themselves for training and enjoyed more days off than any players in the league.

'We had a team meeting on a Friday – when Clough would often keep us all waiting because he was playing squash – and we would perhaps talk for a maximum of two minutes, usually about a goal we had conceded. Clough would then say: 'You, do this; you, dozy bugger, do that; and you, stay there.' End of problem. We never discussed the way the other team might play, who they had in the side or anything like that. He might say to John Robertson: 'I want you to play a little deeper this week,' but that would be all. We wouldn't bother about tactics because we felt we could beat anyone and that they should be worrying about us. It was just a case of going out and playing,' said Ian Bowyer.

Clough was far more worried about the mental state of his players and he would adopt what must have seemed to outsiders some ludicrously unprofessional methods to keep his players relaxed before a big game. On one occasion, Forest were due to play the second leg of a UEFA Cup match against Celtic. The first match had ended 0–0 and Celtic were expected to win handsomely in front of their passionate fans at Parkhead. As the Forest team were being taken from the airport to their hotel, Clough ordered the bus to stop outside the pub owned by the Celtic manager, David Hay. The team had a few drinks, Clough charged the bill to Hay, and then left. The following day they trained very lightly for half an hour, played in the evening, won 2–1 and went home. Even before cup finals Clough was not averse to getting players out of bed late in the evening and forcing them down to the bar.

Not surprisingly perhaps, Clough's idiosyncratic ways drive real coaches to distraction. They cut right across traditional coaching methods, yet they produce results, extraordinary results. 'So who is to say they aren't the right methods?', asks Don Howe, one of the most respected coaches in the game. 'My way of doing things is to work and work and work, morning and afternoon if I have to, until they become better players. In my view, that is the only way they will become better players. If we have been beaten, I will work them harder. Clough would probably just give them a little five-a-side and then send them home. But if on the Saturday his team beats my team, which one is right?' said Howe.

The Clough routine on a Saturday was not exactly out of the FA book of good management, either. He would come into the dressing-room at about 2:30 after playing squash; at 2:45 he would be showered and changed, the players would ask how his squash had gone and then, with about ten minutes to go to kick-off, he would give his team-talk. 'I don't know how he did it,' says Woodcock, 'but by kick-off you were ready to run through brick walls for him.'

Anderson felt no different. An article in *Shoot* magazine at the start of the 1977-78 season was headlined: 'I owe it all to Brian Clough – says Forest's exciting young full-back Viv Anderson.' In it Anderson is quoted as saying: 'He (Clough) is a fair man and he helps you a lot – especially the young lads like Tony Woodcock and myself. For instance, he has made me tackle more and has given me more confidence to move forward. He definitely brings the best out of players – as is evident with Peter Withe, whose full potential has been shown at Forest, and John Robertson, who has come on tremendously. Along with Peter Taylor, he really gets you going on Saturdays and the players are enjoying their football now more than ever before.'

Apart from highlighting one of the enduring weaknesses in his game – his tackling – and producing one of the great footballing understatements of all time ('John Robertson has come on tremendously') the article reflects the wide-eyed innocence of the 22-year-old: new to the First Division, new to success, disbelieving. It also hits one or two nails gently on the head. Being one of Clough's boys did give the players extraordinary inner confidence. If Anderson could take one Cloughian phrase with him to his grave, it would be, 'If you weren't good enough, you wouldn't be in the team.' It's as standard a piece of managerial jargon as you are ever likely to hear, except that in Clough's case it was true, and the players knew it. And if you were good enough for Clough, you were good enough for anyone.

In his excellent diary of a year at Arsenal, called *Inside Soccer*, Tony Woodcock admits that after one game he felt inwardly that many of the players could have given more, himself included. That is some admission for a professional sportsman, who is paid handsomely to give 100 per cent all the time. Woodcock, an introvert who needs to be consciously motivated rather more than a character like Anderson, also felt that the lack of effort was down to Don Howe who threatened to drop players but never actually did so. Some players knew they would be picked every week, wrote Woodcock, and that bred complacency and the inconsistency which plagued Arsenal throughout those years. Complacency was never part of the set-up at Forest, consistency was everything. Consistency of method, of players, of belief – those were the cornerstones of Clough's success at Forest. If Clough thought you were not good enough or not giving enough, that was that, internationals included. In fact, there was a feeling that as a man not averse to creating a bit of controversy, the bigger the player the more he would jump at the chance to drop him. 'The only thing we were frightened of was giving less than 100 per cent,' as Trevor Francis said.

'With Clough, you never knew you were going to be in the team,' added Anderson. 'I remember once that he had put the team sheet up with my name on it. We had gone back to the hotel for a meal and a sleep before going to the ground. At the ground, I got changed into my kit and was just preparing to play when Clough said: 'You, you're not playing,' and I didn't play. You never knew you were going to play until you went out onto the field. I think it might have changed a bit now because he has less scope for making changes. At Arsenal, perhaps too many knew they were going to be in the team. Take Alan Smith, for example. They have to justify paying £800,000 for him him, so they keep playing him. With Clough, he would recognize he had made a mistake and that would be it,' said Anderson. No one had an absolute right to be in the team.

For Anderson's own development, the important thing about Clough's discipline was that it went far beyond the outer image of short back-and-sides and team blazer. Forest players were expected to be disciplined all through. There was no room for shirking and there was no room for sensitivity, not even about the colour of your skin, as Anderson found out fairly early in his career under Clough. 'I was substitute at Carlisle and Clough told me to get warmed up, so I did the usual thing, running up and down the touchline. When I got back into the dug-out, Clough asked me why I had done all my exercises with my back to the crowd. I told him that they had been giving me some stick, so he told me to go back out there and face them.'

'Go and call him a white bastard, then kick him back,' was Clough's robust response to racial taunts on the field. Don Howe commented, 'That sort of attitude was very good for Viv, I think. It was rather like a father/son relationship, with Clough saying: "Don't come running to me about it, son, sort it out yourself." And Viv did. At Arsenal, if he was given any stick, he would just laugh about it and then make sure he played twice as hard.'

Brought up in a disciplined household under the stern eye of his parents, Anderson was getting a priceless discipline at work as well, a discipline which did not just involve looking the part, but playing the part too. Clough expected total commitment to producing your best on the field for Forest not just every now and then, but every single game. 'Cloughie drilled it into you. Concentration in everything –

passing, heading, tackling, everything. In the early days, I used to give the ball away with silly passes; I wasn't consistent and I was dropped for it. Everything, physical and mental, has to be at a peak for those ninety minutes you play. Every aspect you could possibly think of as a footballer has got to be right for that time to achieve anything. You can get away with one or two having an off-day, but eight or nine others have to be spot on. Look at Liverpool – consistent week in, week out, it's remarkable. We had that at Forest, we didn't at Arsenal and we don't at Manchester United at the moment. No pattern, lack of concentration – it's probably a bit of both, but if you have an easy-easy attitude then you are not going to win anything.'

Anyone not willing to submit himself to the tyranny, like the colourful Stan Bowles, soon found that the door was closed. In return for the commitment, Clough and Taylor promised just one thing: success. If you wanted it, you came to Forest and did as you were told; if you didn't, well, Forest wouldn't want you anyway. When in February 1979 they wanted to persuade Birmingham's Trevor Francis to reject a lucrative deal with Coventry, which also included summer seasons with Jimmy Hill's Detroit Express team in the States, and to sign for Forest instead, Clough appealed not to his pocket but to his desire for success. 'Show us your medals,' he invited Francis. Francis couldn't and came to Forest, being rewarded for his decision by a medal for the European Cup inside four months and twenty games.

The Francis transfer was also interesting as an illustration of Clough's enormous ego, according to Anderson. 'He wanted to be the first manager to pay £1m for a player. It appealed to his ego. No doubt about it.' With Francis, though, it lead to a bad footballing misjudgement. The bone of contention was whether Francis would be allowed to honour his summer contract with Detroit, which could mean him missing the first few games of the season and first two rounds of the European Cup. Clough initially said 'No', but when he saw the player was hesitating about coming to Forest, uncharacteristically he relented. Francis has admitted that he had already been persuaded to come to Forest anyway; if Clough had held out a little longer, he would have got his man on his own terms. But he didn't, and the following season Francis returned to Forest with a groin injury, which kept him out of the side and in the headlines for two months. At one point, Clough wanted Detroit to pay his wages.

Even to those like Anderson who have played with him for a long time, Clough is a complex character. Yet his views on how football should be played are alarmingly simple. He is not a coach, has never pretended to be, has a high disdain for anyone who is and shows it by reducing the game to a minimum of basic rules: pass the ball to a member of your own team, use the full width of the pitch, be strong down the backbone of the side – goalkeeper, centre-halves, centre-forward – play the ball to feet up front, centre-forwards to hold the ball and turn or wait for support from the midfield, centre-halves to kick it and head it with no fancy asides, crosses to be pinpointed, corners always taken short. That was about it.

'Clough had about seven or eight points that he would make,' said Martin O'Neill. 'If you adhered to those you would end up a better player. The other day, against Charlton, Forest were winning 2–1 with three minutes to go. Tommy Gaynor (a young Forest forward) gave the ball away and Charlton scored. Clough went straight into the dug-out, picked up the number 10 board and stuck it right in front of Gaynor's face to show he was being taken off. Gaynor will remember that for the rest of his life, and rightly so. It's criminal. You're playing a professional game and you go and give the ball away. It's a business; you're not playing for enjoyment any more – managers only say that as an afterthought – you're playing for your livelihood.

'I mean, if you are 1–0 up with a minute to go and you have the ball, you don't go steaming down the wing and whip in a cross so that the other side can clear it and start another attack. You hang on to it and don't give it away. You might bore people to death, but if you won ten games 1–0 and were top of the league, you'd get a full house for the eleventh game, but if you lost ten games 11-10, you'd be bottom of the league and no one would come. Unfortunately, that's life.

'It took me a long time to learn those basic things, a long time from being in love with the game to playing it at a professional level. It has nothing to do with enjoyment and I would defy a lot of players playing top-class football to say that they go out and enjoy the game. The only time you enjoy a game is when it's 5–0 with one minute to go and you've scored all five.'

O'Neill never entirely fitted in to Clough's mould of the ideal footballer. Clough's ideal footballer was John McGovern, a man who worked hard, did as he was told and who was entirely indebted to Clough for his success. O'Neill worked hard, didn't always do as he was told and reckoned himself a good enough player to make a success

1. Viv's mother and father pictured shortly after their arrival in Nottingham in 1954

2. With Debra in the garden of their home in Nottingham just before the move to London

3. If Forest were rank outsiders for the Championship in 1977–78, they weren't exactly favourites for the European Cup the following year either. After wins against Liverpool and Cologne, the final against Malmo proved an anti-climax, but no one seemed to mind. The cast (*from back left*): Anderson, Shilton, Woods, McGovern, Bowyer, Needham, Francis, Clark, O'Hare. (*Front*): Lloyd (partially hidden), Robertson, Woodcock, Jimmy Gordon (coach, standing), Birtles and Burns

4. Ten white faces, one black: an historic debut for England on a frozen night at Wembley, 29th November 1978. Old campaigner Dave Watson is in front, old friend and Forest team-mate Tony Woodcock behind

5. 'Cloughie was the straight man, Pete the clown. Together they were brilliant'

6. Why Anderson became a footballer. Bowled second ball for 0 during a match against Mexico City Cricket Club on England's summer tour in 1985

7. 'John Robertson was fat and lazy, but he had a brilliant football brain.' Anderson tries to impose a full-back's brawn, England *v.* Scotland, Wembley, 1981

8. The extension at work: Clive Allen of Tottenham is the victim

9. Another medal for the collection: leading the victory lap after Arsenal's defeat of Liverpool in the Littlewoods Cup, 1986

10. Glenn Hoddle: 'His skill on the ball takes your breath away. Why hasn't he got 100 England caps?'

11. The full-back's dream: a rare international goal for Anderson, the eighth of England's

12. Paid to defend: Anderson helps Paul McGrath repel a Tottenham attack during his first season with Manchester United, Old Trafford, 1987

13. The scrawny kid from Nottingham . . . and 14 years on, the complete professional at United

of the game with or without Clough. Clough, says O'Neill, could have got an extra 30 per cent out of him with a little more praise and a little less kicking. 'If you're a manager, you can only play eleven players at any one time, so you're always going to have five or six who aren't happy. I used to argue a lot with Brian and I knew he thought that I thought I was a better player than I was – if you can comprehend the Irish. But Brian Clough taught me how to play the game in a professional way. You can go out and play a Sunday league match and enjoy it because there is not a lot at stake. But professional football is played for a living and if you are going to play the game for a living you couldn't get a better teacher than Clough.

'Clough knows that football is basically a team game but that to make a good team you have to get the best out of eleven individuals. At Forest I was the exception because I believe he didn't get the best out of me.'

While Clough's dislike – perhaps distrust would be a better word – of O'Neill was unproductive, it was at least understandable. Managers tend not to take kindly to highly articulate footballers arguing with them. Less easy to understand was his dislike of Peter Withe, an old-fashioned centre-forward, who fitted exactly the job description Clough outlined for his centre-forwards – big, strong, brave and able to hold the ball all day and all night, if need be. Withe was not a prolific goalscorer, but he was an essential part of the team, part of the solid backbone that Clough liked to have in his sides. Anderson could not understand Clough's attitude to the amiable Liverpudlian, either.

'Googie (after Googie Withers the actress) never had the best of times at Forest. Clough was always moaning at him. He never fancied him – I don't know why because he played brilliantly for us and he proved what a good player he is when he went on to Aston Villa. For some reason, though, Clough victimized him, almost. I remember after the Ipswich match when Googie had scored all four goals, he wanted us to sign the ball so that he could keep it. Clough refused. "You'll get the ball when you learn to play with it properly," he said. We got the ball for him anyway, but it's a strange attitude.

'Another time, Peter injured his ankle in a tackle just before half-time and he was really struggling. But when he came in at half-time, Clough said: "Don't think you're f— well coming off, get back out there." So the physio put a piece of strapping round his boot and he went back out. He hobbled around for all the second half. It was pointless, but Clough had to make his mark. He once made Calvin Plummer play most of a half with what turned out to be a broken foot. Some of the things he did were very close to the borderline of madness. That's just how he was.'

In contrast, John McGovern, a player of mediocre talent but prodigious work-rate, was praised constantly. 'Captain, you were brilliant,' Clough would say to him. It was almost as if Clough was deliberately championing the role of the underdog, the bits-and-pieces player, over his better-known and more talented team-mates. McGovern was a simple footballer and Clough liked simple football. He didn't want heroics, he wanted a player to pass it to a red shirt, he wanted his defenders to get the ball and give it to someone who was being paid to distribute it, he wanted the centre-forward to hold the ball and wait for support from the midfield, he wanted Robertson on the left and O'Neill and Anderson down the right to stay wide and get behind defences. Above all, he wanted his players to perform to the limits of their ability every game. McGovern did that, filling the hole in front of the back four so that the opposition could not exploit Lloyd's and Burns's lack of pace, and was rewarded with one of the most successful careers in the game.

On a different level, the same could be said of Anderson. At the start of the 1977–78 season, Anderson was a raw novice, with plenty of ability but precious little confidence in it. By his bullying ('I'm portrayed as a bully, but I'm just a bloke doing a job. I only bully if I need to,' as Clough once said), by his manner, by his autocracy, by his success, Clough turned Anderson into an international and gave him a discipline which has stayed with him throughout his career. Tony Woodcock summarized Clough's influence thus: 'I suppose the best thing I can say about him is that he built a successful team and put me in it.'

Let Viv Anderson have the last word. 'I just look upon him as Cloughie, be-all and end-all. Not someone I like, but someone I admire and respect. If I went back and he said: "Hello, Viv, how are you?" and was all over me, I'd be thinking hard what's round the corner. Everything you ever heard about him, he lives up to. He's unique. There's nothing more to say.'

SIX

# TRAVELS IN EUROPE

If the media scepticism about Forest's ability had been largely dispelled by the time they picked up the league championship trophy in April 1978, it surfaced again as soon as the draw was made for the European Cup the following season. England had two representatives: Liverpool as holders and Nottingham Forest as League champions. Before the draw Bob Paisley, Liverpool's manager, expressed the view that Forest posed the biggest threat to his team's chances of winning their third successive European Cup. Not even Paisley's wise old head could have anticipated the cruelty of the first-round draw, but he must have regretted those words as soon as he heard it: Forest v. Liverpool. There was a universal air of disbelief in English football and a huge sigh of relief elsewhere in Europe – at least one of the English clubs would fall by the wayside.

Understandably most of the football writers predicted that Forest would be the ones left behind. The first leg of the tie would be their first European match, Liverpool's 98th (not counting two Super Cup matches), of which they had won 56, drawn 18 and lost 23. They had been through a long process of European education and, in the last two seasons, had emerged as top of the class. Forest, on the other hand, had come straight into the sixth form. In addition, Liverpool had discarded their frailties of the previous season and had begun the season in style, while Forest, although continuing where they had left off the previous season, were not quite displaying the same conviction. They had sold their centre-forward, Withe, and had not yet settled on a suitable replacement. Goals were more hard to come by. The Saturday before the tie, against Arsenal, they had experimented with a new centre-forward, Garry Birtles, a non-league player who had only played one previous league match for Forest. There was nothing much in that to frighten Souness, Thompson and company. Above all, the tie had fallen nicely for Liverpool: away leg first, home leg second – that was the way they liked it.

But there must have been nagging doubts. Liverpool had not beaten Forest in four matches the previous season and they had only scored once. What's more, Forest had outslogged them in the replayed League Cup final in what had turned out to be a dress rehearsal for the two-leg European Cup match. In the end Forest had won by a dubious penalty decision. Such strokes of luck were usually Liverpool's preserve and the fact that Forest had muscled in on their territory can have done little for their psychological well-being. The Liverpool bogey, which has loomed large over most European sides, meant nothing to Forest. 'So what' was their legitimate reply to the doom-laden sign 'This is Anfield' over the players' tunnel. No, deep down, it was Liverpool, not Forest, who had most to fear.

At least Forest had enough respect to change their ways. For once it was not just a case of going out and playing. Clough had a plan. Instead of allowing Woodcock to exploit his usual channel down the inside-left position, the Forest manager withdrew him and played him more down the right so that he could run from deep positions, and Gemmill, who had been dropped for the last league match, was brought back on the right side of midfield in place of O'Neill to stop Alan Kennedy getting forward. It was one of the few times in the three years of success at Forest that the system was changed. Clough also gambled on the pace and the inexperience of Birtles, a player whom he had once said had only been kept at Forest because he made a good squash partner. The Clough/Taylor partnership had nearly come apart over their differing assessment of Birtles: Taylor had seen something he liked in the diffident young striker from Long Eaton; Clough could see nothing at all.

By the end of the first leg against Liverpool, he had changed his mind. Birtles scored the first goal after Woodcock had broken through down his unfavoured right side, and made the second for Barrett three minutes from the end. It was the turning point of the tie, the real beginning of Forest's long journey through Europe.

In *The Times* the goal was simply but accurately described: 'Barrett cleared, Birtles collected the ball on the left wing and beat Case and Thompson with the ease of a veteran. He centred and Woodcock cleverly headed back across the goal for Barrett, who had followed up at speed to volley in a marvellous significant goal on a night that blew fresh heart into Forest.' Not only was it a goal of classic Forest simplicity, it changed the psychological balance of the tie.

'They would have settled for a 1–0. No doubt about that,' said Ian Bowyer. 'If we had only taken a one-goal lead to Anfield, it would have been very difficult. But the second goal put a totally different complexion on the game. We were going to run the gauntlet at Anfield anyway, but with two goals you have a cushion and that was important psychologically.'

Liverpool had, it seemed, almost become a victim of their own experience. They tried to calm things down, play at European rather than league pace. Forest had no such refinement. They only had one gear, flat out, and they pressurized Liverpool into uncharacteristic errors. Indeed, so flustered were they by the end that Phil Thompson was reduced to verbal taunts of 'Wait till we get you at Anfield' as the players left the field.

If Forest's nerve had been tested at the City Ground in the first leg, their character was given an awesome battering at Anfield. The team knew that it would be and were ready for it. In the last game of the 1977–78 season, they had come away with a meaningless goalless draw. Unashamedly, they set their stall out to do the same in front of 52,000 passionate Merseysiders, and succeeded. They crowded the midfield, defended a line just outside their penalty-area and rarely let the Liverpool forwards get round the back in a performance that was a tribute to their determination and collective ability to defend. In particular, the battle between the former Liverpool favourite Larry Lloyd and Kenny Dalglish was conclusively won by Lloyd. 'Larry used to play Dalglish better than anyone. Instead of staying absolutely tight and allowing Dalglish to turn him, Larry used to give him a yard or two and just hold him up, not allowing him to turn. He played Dalglish brilliantly that night.' Only once did the little Scot break through, and then his header was cleared off the line by Anderson. It proved to be their only real chance. In the end, Forest emerged from the fray quite comfortably in possession of their two-goal lead and a place in the second round. Indeed, they could even have sneaked a win if the referee had not disallowed legitimate claims for a penalty when Anderson's shot was blocked by Thompson's hand. Typically, Anderson remembers more about the unorthodox build-up to the match than the game itself.

'We got on the bus for the ground, but had to wait and wait for Cloughie. Eventually, we set off at about six o'clock. His explanation was that everybody would be in the ground by the time we arrived so we would have a clear run. In the end, we arrived only about forty-five minutes before kick-off. On the bus, Clough handed round beer and wine. It was incredible – we might have been playing a friendly. But it worked. We didn't really have time to get nervous about the atmosphere and we were very relaxed. About twenty minutes after the end of the game, we were back on the bus and on our way back to Nottingham.

'On reflection, though it didn't seem like it at the time, the tie against Liverpool was probably the best one we could have had. If we had been drawn against some unknown East European side, we wouldn't have had any idea what to expect. With Liverpool, we just played the same way as we always did. When we eventually did have to play in Europe, we had the confidence of knowing that we had beaten the holders, so we had no need to fear anybody at all while the other European clubs knew that we had beaten the mighty Liverpool and had therefore transferred their fear of Liverpool to us. That made it easier.'

Such was the confidence in English football at the time that, with their highest hurdle safely jumped, Forest were widely expected to have a relatively carefree run to the trophy. That feeling was enhanced when they comfortably disposed of the Greek champions AEK Athens in the second round. The basis of their victory was laid in the first leg in Athens when goals from McGovern and Birtles in the first half gave them a priceless 2–1 advantage for the second leg when they comprehensively finished their task with a 5–1 win, Anderson himself scoring the best goal of the night with a 25-yard shot.

Elsewhere, results fell nicely for Forest. Rangers had already beaten Juventus, Real Madrid had been beaten by the Swiss side, Grasshoppers, and Bruges, finalists from the previous season, had also gone. Only the German side, Cologne, seemed to stand in the way of another English victory in the European Cup and after a tough tie against Grasshoppers when only two goals in the last four minutes of the first leg ensured a 5–2 aggregate victory which looked more comfortable on paper than in fact, Forest were duly drawn to meet the German champions in the semi-final.

In many ways, the match against Cologne, rather than either of the two finals, was the highlight of Forest's 21-game run in the European Cup. Ask any of the players which game they remember best and it will probably not be the finals but the one against Cologne. Any match against a German side has an extra dimension but, with the ageing master Hennes Weisweiler in charge of Cologne pitted against the ebullient and relatively inexperienced partnership of Clough and Taylor, the confrontation was as much off the field as on it. Cologne had Dieter Muller, Cullmann and Schuster, Forest would be without

Anderson, who was booked in the previous tie against Grasshoppers and therefore suspended, and Trevor Francis, bought just a few months before for £1m. The first leg at Nottingham began disastrously for Forest, as Tony Woodcock recalled: 'Peter Taylor had given us the run-down on them. He told us that the goalkeeper couldn't catch the ball, they had no one who could shoot and no pace at all. So we went out thinking they would be no problem. After twenty minutes, they had run all over us, we were 2–0 down and wondering if Pete had watched the right team, but we gradually managed to get back into the game and actually got ahead until they equalized in the last ten minutes.'

It was a brilliant match marked by two rarities: first a mistake by Shilton, and second a goal by a Japanese player. Forest had fought back to lead 3–2 when a 25-yard shot by the substitute Okudera, one of the few Japanese players in European football, crept under Shilton's body and into the net. Needless to say, the tabloids could not resist such a moment. 'Jap sub sinks Forest' roared one headline. It was a view shared by most of Fleet Street. 'Although Forest's prospects of survival look slim indeed they are far better than they were at eight o'clock. Cologne were deprived of a virtual walk-over by Forest's undying spirit, the commendable skill of Robertson and Bowyer's power and determination,' wrote Donald Saunders in the *Daily Telegraph*, concluding his typically balanced report with a prediction: 'I have little doubt that when battle is resumed Cologne will add one or two more to the healthy bag of goals.'

'It was probably the most exciting game I've ever played in. But people who should have known better wrote us off,' said Bowyer. It was perhaps not surprising. Even for Forest, an away win in Cologne seemed a remote prospect, though typically neither Clough nor Peter Taylor would entertain defeat. After the match, Clough predicted that Cologne would not score. It seemed one of his more irrational remarks, but in fact Clough was just expressing the general air of optimism in the Forest dressing-room. 'We knew we had played badly and yet had still managed a draw,' commented Woodcock. 'We were never going to defend as poorly again so we really thought we could win the second leg, but we were about the only people in the country who did.' Having been forced to sit-out the first leg in the stand, Anderson was recalled for the second leg a fortnight later. The omens for the match were good for Forest. They had refound the goal touch which had deserted them in the league, thrashing Chelsea 6–0 ten days before. At the same time, Cologne were on the wrong end of a 5–1 beating by Bayern Munich. Forest's preparation for the match was predictably downbeat. They arrived in Cologne, went for a few walks, sank a few beers, did a little training and then produced the classic away performance.

Psychologically and tactically it is easier to go into a tie knowing you have to win. If a draw will do, then the equation becomes confused. Do you hold on to to what you've got, or go out for more? Countless teams have failed to solve that particular puzzle. Only a 4–4 draw would have done for Forest and that was out of the question. They had to win. Instructed not to give away a goal before half-time and then to score midway through the second half, Forest did as they were told, stifling the German team before Bowyer snatched the winner with a header from a corner. Even then only a finger-tip save by Shilton from a 25-yard drive by the Cologne full-back, Konopka, saved the tie and justified Clough's bold prediction. Forest had reached their first European Cup final.

While Forest had been enjoying their hair-raising adventures in Europe, the career of their young full-back had taken a giant step forward. Being constantly in the limelight had done little harm to Anderson's international claims. In the previous summer, he had been selected to tour the Far East with the England B team, drawing rave notices from fellow players and the B team manager, Bobby Robson, as they completed an unbeaten seven-match tour.

'There are at least seven players on this tour who will disappoint me if they do not become regular England first-team players, and you can include Anderson among them. I think he is a certainty,' said Robson.

'He still has to tighten up a bit defensively,' said Joe Corrigan. 'But he's a smashing lad and definitely a full international of the not-so-distant future.' John Hollins echoed that view: 'He gets better all the time. And a season in Europe with Forest will really polish off the rough edges. If he continues to improve as he has been, he'll be an England man for a very long time.'

Anderson's international star was clearly on the rise and he lost nothing in the inevitable comparison with Phil Neal, the regular England full-back, during the two European Cup matches against Liverpool. The man himself was not aware that he was being measured for his England shirt.

'Being selected for the Far East tour so shortly after my debut for the England Under-21s was obviously encouraging. It meant I was at least going in the right direction. But the possibility of being the first coloured player to play for England had never really entered my head, though I was asked about it a few times. I wanted to be picked as a player, not as a *coloured* player. Forest playing in Europe was a constant reminder to people of what I could do so I was lucky in that respect. If you are playing against good continental opposition regularly that can only help you prepare for international football. But I don't think I ever consciously viewed it in those terms.'

If Anderson didn't, others certainly did. Commenting after the Liverpool tie, David Miller, now chief sports correspondent of *The Times*, then writing for the *Express*, had this to say: 'The eclipse of the champions was accomplished with the exact defensive efficiency that has been the hallmark of Liverpool themselves and Leeds for over a decade. And none was more efficient than Anderson, who has emerged as a highly qualified rival to his opposite number on that historic night, Phil Neal. The timing of Anderson's tackling and interceptions is now as clean and sharp as almost any player in the First Division, reminding one in certain moments even of Bobby Moore.' High praise indeed for a player who could not have been less reminiscent of the former England captain in colour and build. Miller also noted the importance of a European Cup run in the development of players like Anderson and Woodcock and hoped the England manager Ron Greenwood would too.

Greenwood needed little prompting from the press to bring Anderson into his international plans. A month after the second-round tie against AEK Athens, Anderson was included in the team against Czechoslovakia and duly reached the top rung of the ladder on a half-frozen pitch at Wembley in late November. Just over five months later, still only twenty-two, Anderson had a European Cup medal to put alongside his first international cap in the glass showcase at his parents' council house on the Clifton Estate. No wonder he said at the time that things were happening very quickly.

Unfortunately, as so often happens, neither occasion quite matched up to expectations. The international was not a classic and, though Anderson acquitted himself capably on a difficult night for defenders, he did not match up to his own high standards. 'Nothing more than adequate' was his description of his performance ten years later. The phrase could easily be used to describe the 1978–79 European Cup final, a low-key affair between two teams not exactly ringing with European tradition, Nottingham Forest and Malmo.

The Swedish side had failed to progress beyond the second round in seven previous attempts in the competition but, under the astute guidance of Bob Houghton, who had played without distinction for Brighton and Fulham before moving to Scandinavia, had disposed of Monaco, Dynamo Kiev, Wisla Krakow and WAC Austria on their way to an unlikely final in Munich. This was a situation new to Forest. They had thrived for so long on the will to prove everyone wrong that they had forgotten what it was like to be expected to win. After beating the champions of West Germany, Switzerland, Greece and England along the way, the part-timers from Malmo were not expected to give much trouble. Clough did his best to dispel any complacency, predicting that his team would have to play as well as they did against Athens and 'nearly as well' as they did in the second leg of the match against Cologne to beat the Swedes. It is doubtful whether he or his players really believed that and, their disbelief was justified. Forest won all right, through a rare headed goal by Trevor Francis just before half-time, but the performance and the match, as so often in European Cup finals, was an anti-climax.

Anderson recalled, 'I don't think we were ever in danger of losing because they just seemed happy to defend even when they were 1–0 down. They were hard to break down but we were disappointed with ourselves even though we had won the European Cup. I remember after we had collected the trophy and done the lap of honour, we sat in the dressing-room quite quietly. There wasn't the buzz that there was after the Cologne match. But Ian Bowyer pointed out that we hadn't just won the Cup tonight, we'd won it with our performances over the previous six months. He was right, but it was difficult to see it in those terms.'

Clough, who signed a new four-year contract immediately after the final and then flew off to resume his family holiday in Crete, might have reflected rather further back than the previous six months. Two and a half years before as his side was losing to Oldham in the Second Division and Liverpool was preparing to win their first European Cup, Clough had gone to watch Enderby play Long Eaton. The object of his attention was a spindly carpet-layer named Garry Birtles. Against his better judgement, Clough was persuaded to pay £2000 for him. At the time, Clough thought Birtles overpriced, but not for the first or last time he was wrong. In his first seven European Cup games, Birtles scored six goals. A gem at the bottom of a slagheap; it's the football manager's dream.

'When he went to Manchester United, he was the best centre-forward in the country by far. He could do everything – hold the ball up, turn and run at defenders, score goals. Peter Withe was very good for us, good in the air and better than people thought on the ground, John O'Hare was great to play with because he could hold the ball all night so that you had time to get forward, but Birtles was the best centre-forward I have ever seen. A fabulous, fabulous footballer.' Anderson is rarely so fulsome in his praise. Birtles must have been good.

Forest did a double the following year, too, winning the European Cup and the League Cup. In the latter they came from one goal down to beat Southampton, though Anderson did not play because of injury. But in the league they finished second to Liverpool. So, once again, both English clubs went into the draw for the first round of the European Cup in the 1979–80 season.

In a sense, Forest's second success in the European Cup was even more remarkable than the first. Measured against the likes of Real Madrid, Ajax of Amsterdam or Hamburg, their pedigree did not stand the test, nor did their league form. Woodcock had gone, Clark had retired; Asa Hartford, Stan Bowles and, on loan, Charlie George had been brought in. Times were beginning to change and yet the results just kept flowing – at least in Europe. In the league, they lost six away games in succession. But Forest as ever spurned the easy way to the top, losing at home to Dynamo Berlin and having to pull out what has been described as one of the great away perfomances in the European Cup in the second leg to win 3–1 in Berlin. In the semi-final, they were battered remorselessly by the Dutch champions Ajax during the last twenty minutes of the second leg but held on to their 2–1 aggregate lead to reach the final for the second year running, this time against Hamburg and Kevin Keegan.

'I'm convinced Clough thought we were going to get hammered,' said Anderson, 'because we went away to Majorca and, though we trained every day, we were out drinking every night. People couldn't believe that we were supposed to be playing in the European Cup final. I remember one day Peter Shilton wanted to go out for a training session and there wasn't anywhere to go. The only place he could find was a little island in the middle of a road, so he went and practised there – three days before a European Cup final.'

Quite apart from that, Forest's build-up was anything but smooth. Trevor Francis was injured and his replacement was an inexperienced

18-year-old, Gary Mills. Stan Bowles, drafted into Forest's midfield halfway through the season, had simply failed to turn up when the team left for Majorca, so Forest only had four substitutes instead of their allotted five. But, back in their role as perpetual underdogs, they were happy. Hamburg had Hrubesch and Kaltz, Magath and Keegan. They had won their previous rounds comfortably, including the semi-final against Real Madrid. They were *expected* to win; Forest *had* to win.

'This match was effectively our season and it showed on the faces of the players as we went to the Bernabeu Stadium,' said Bowyer. 'We weren't usually as tense, but we knew that this was important not just for us but for the club. If we didn't win, we were effectively out of Europe because we had lost the League Cup and hadn't qualified through our league position. With a new stand being built, it was vital that we got back into Europe for financial reasons alone.'

Forest achieved their end, John Robertson scoring in the first half, but the means were not pretty. Like Malmo the year before, they unashamedly set out to contain. They packed the midfield and left Birtles as the sole striker. Keegan was ruggedly handled by Burns and retreated into midfield, Forest defended doggedly, Shilton kept superbly and Forest retained the European Cup. The critics were not impressed. The Germans denounced it as 'Blitzkrieg' football, while the impartial Spanish football writers called it simply 'soulless'.

Brian Glanville, distinguished football correspondent of the *Sunday Times*, lamented the lack of individualism and the demise of Total Football. He accused Clough of 'tactical cowardice'. 'Italian football is riddled with it, it was Arsenal's undoing this season when it came to the crunch, Forest showed it in Madrid. Having saluted their unquestionably superb achievement in winning the European title twice in a row, having acknowledged the excellence of Shilton, the prowess of Lloyd, Burns, O'Neill, Birtles and Robertson, it must still be said that their second-half strategy was a craven one, worthy of Juventus at their worst.'

Forest had gained the upper hand just before half-time, Glanville argued, but 'came out for the second half a different and diminished team, resigned to a battle of attrition . . . The team, the tactics, essentially gambled on the brilliance of Shilton, and the gamble succeeded.' For once, Glanville was arguing from a position of weakness. The gamble, as he said, had succeeded. There was nothing more to say. Keegan shook his head sadly at the end: 'Forest are uncanny in the way they make you play to their strengths. They block off the middle with so many players that they force you to go wide. Then they have two central defenders and a goalkeeper who are outstanding at dealing with crosses.'

By playing to their strengths and getting other teams to do the same, by the good old-fashioned virtues of pride and patriotism, by playing just as they had week after week in the league, Forest had joined the great names of European football – Real Madrid, Liverpool, Ajax, Bayern, Benfica and Inter Milan – in retaining the European Cup. 'Our style was suited to European football,' explained Anderson. 'We were always a counter-attacking team and so we were always very dangerous away from home, which is the secret of playing in Europe. The only difference was that we had to learn to be patient and to take the chances when they came. You were never going to get as many chances as you would in a league match, so you had to put them away. It's the same in any international football.'

Shortly after Forest had completed their lap of honour, they were changed and whisked back to their mountain retreat thirty miles from Madrid. Outside the stadium, a small group of players' wives and girl friends were left to celebrate on their own. Typically, in their hour of triumph, Clough wanted the players to himself. Perhaps he knew it would be for the last time. Within a year, Bowyer, O'Neill, Birtles, Gemmill, Burns and Lloyd had gone and Anderson had turned from office boy to senior partner almost overnight. The following season Forest lost to CSKA Sofia in the first round, league form was patchy. Success had come quickly to Forest; it disappeared almost as fast.

SEVEN

# DISENCHANTED FOREST

Liverpool are not the best loved team in the land; they win far too often for that. But they are the most respected, both inside and outside the game, for their consistency, that quality which is at the very heart of the English football league. But it's not just their consistency over two or three seasons that causes a player like Anderson to shake his head in wonder. It is their extraordinary ability to keep winning things for decades, to change the façade without showing the cracks. Every club is supposed to experience periods of transition as one team gets too old and the next learns the art of winning. At Anfield, the production line never stops. While one team is winning out on the pitch, the next is being designed in the Research and Development Department, otherwise known as the boot room. Change at Liverpool has always been gradual. Ian Rush, for example, was bought for a huge figure at the time, £300,000, from Chester and played in the reserves for three years before he was considered ready to score goals in the first team.

At Forest, whether because of Clough or the players, because of money or because the club had no experience of sustained success over a long period, it did not quite happen like that. By nature, neither Clough nor Taylor were inclined to do things gradually. They worked by instinct and hunch, not by a system; and so the Forest team quickly and surely disintegrated.

There had been indications that Clough and Taylor's judgement of a player was not always infallible. In July 1979 they bought Asa Hartford from Manchester City for £400,000. Sixty-three days later they sold him for the same figure to Everton. At the time Peter Taylor said: 'Asa is one helluva player and he will fit in very well for someone. But we can't alter our pattern of play for him.' As Anderson points out, Hartford had been around the game long enough for everyone to know what sort of a player he was. 'Asa doesn't pass the ball,' Malcolm Allison had once said, 'he only lends it to you.'

'They bought Asa to replace Gemmill because, like Archie, he was a quick little player,' said Anderson. 'But they wanted him to start playing long balls and Asa had never played a long ball in his life. So within a few months he was on his way again. I remember it was at the start of one season and we saw Asa heading off out of the hotel. We asked him where he was going and he said: "To have talks with Everton." We thought he was joking, but he wasn't.'

The Hartford blunder took on more significance during the next few years as the European Cup team was sold off one after another. October 1980: Birtles to Manchester United for £1,250,000. January 1981: the faithful Bowyer to Sunderland for £250,000. February 1981: Martin O'Neill to Norwich for the same sum (then on to Manchester City four months later). September 1981: Trevor Francis to Manchester City for £1,200,000. The following month: Burns to Leeds for £400,000. Most of those deals were good business and, by the end of the year, Forest had enough money in the bank to buy Nottingham Town Hall. Instead they bought Justin Fashanu and Ian Wallace for over £2m the pair. And there were other purchases. Mark Proctor: £425,000 from Middlesbrough. Raymondo Ponte: £230,000 from Grasshoppers. Peter Ward: £400,000 from Brighton. Einer Aas: £250,000 from Bayern Munich. Willie Young: £150,000 from Arsenal. For a time, Forest bought and sold players like a street-trader in the Portobello market. But still success eluded them.

Bowyer, O'Neill and Anderson disagree about whether the European Cup side was broken up too early. 'I think we could have gone on and won a few more things with the basis of that side,' said O'Neill. Bowyer had a different view: 'We couldn't have gone on much longer. Football changes so quickly. Only Liverpool seem to progress from one winning team to another without anyone really noticing. But I do think we should have changed the team more gradually. We bought Wallace, Fashanu and Ward for over £2m overall and none of them were anywhere near the class of the previous players like Withe, Woodcock, Francis or Birtles. A lot of people get disillusioned very quickly when you start letting players of that calibre go.' Anderson subscribes more to the Bowyer view, but even he was surprised by the turnover of players. 'A lot of the new players were absolutely amazed at some of the things Cloughie did. Asa was, so was Stan Bowles. Frans Thijssen was bought and the day after his first training session with Forest he read in the newspaper that Clough had said he had made a mistake in buying him. Frans couldn't believe it and after that Clough mucked him about and he left.'

If Wallace and Ward represented mild, though expensive, aberrations in the transfer market, the saga of Justin Fashanu touched the depths of farce. Part tragedy, part comedy, the row between the former Barnardo's boy and the eccentric Forest manager was pure soap opera, though not even the most imaginative scriptwriter could have penned the final scene as Fashanu was escorted from the Forest training ground by the local constabulary The whole episode was played out on the pages of the tabloids and though it must have made good reading in the Forest dressing-room it could not have done much for morale. Fashanu was a more complex and sensitive character than Clough had been used to. A Christian off the field, he was a big, powerful, fearless brute on it, the only player in the league who by sheer physical presence had mastered the awesome pairing of Lloyd and Burns. Clough had not forgotten that and, in August 1981, brought Fashanu to the City Ground. Anderson remembers an early unconventional example of Fashanu's extraordinary power.

'We were rooming together for a pre-season tournament in Spain. In the middle of the night, I was woken up by this great banging on the door. I woke up and there was no sign of Fash and then I noticed the door. It was like someone had gone through it with an axe. Fash had been having a nightmare and smashed the door down with his hands. It was frightening how strong he was.'

Strong or not, Clough never liked Fashanu and Fashanu replied in kind: three goals in thirty-one games. 'It was a clash of personalities from the start. Fash brought his masseur with him. Clough thought he was a poof and kept asking him if he was, which, of course, pleased Fash immensely. He also had weak ankles and used to strap them up, so Clough banned strapping for training. He was merciless in his criticism.' Fashanu eventually moved on to neighbours Notts County for £900,000 less then Clough paid for him. His three goals cost £333,333 each (plus VAT).

'If [Clough] had spent the money and had some of the failures he had at any other club, he would have been sacked straightaway. No question. He would be the first to admit that but he brought Forest success so they stayed loyal through his failures. I never really lost faith in his ability, but I did worry at first about not getting success. After three years of winning everything in sight, you get used to the feeling,' said Anderson.

Players get hooked on the idea of success. Equally, they want to improve their own game by playing with top-class players. Nothing upsets good players more than seeing a manager sell his best players, whatever the business sense. Anderson himself says that when Arsenal made an offer for him in 1984, he was impressed by Don Howe's commitment to winning things, to bringing the best players to Highbury. Fashanu came to Forest on the promise that the club were wanting to build a side and would not be selling their best players; yet Trevor Francis had gone to Manchester City within a month of his arrival.

At close quarters, Anderson honestly believed that Forest were on the verge of winning things again. Ian Bowyer, however, was in a far better position to look at Forest's decline. Transferred to Sunderland, where Frank Clark was assistant manager, in January 1981, he returned to Forest almost exactly a year later. 'The place had changed quite dramatically. A lot of the players had gone, John McGovern was in and out of the team and Shilton had said he would be going in the summer. But they hadn't been replaced with players of the same ability. It wasn't as good a side, and the feel in the dressing-room wasn't the same, either. Whether that was because Clough had got rid of players you could rely on for a good laugh and a joke, or whether it was because the team was not so successful, I don't know, but, from having experienced players who knew their jobs inside out, we'd now got a very young team with players like Stuart Gray, Colin Walsh, Gary Mills and Steve Hodge coming in.

'I think Peter Taylor had a big say in the transfers, certainly in bringing Peter Ward to the club, and it was at the time Clough had been ill. Poor John McGovern was in the side when Clough picked the team and out of it when Taylor picked it and even he, as meek and mild a person as you are ever likely to meet, was beginning to get disgruntled about it. That was sad because John had been a great, great servant of the club. The club was certainly not as happy as when I left.'

Through all the comings and goings, the tantrums and the traumas, Anderson emerged unscathed, ploughing his lonely furrow down the touchlines of the City Ground. Arsenal had made a tentative enquiry about his availibility when his contract was up for renewal in 1982 and there was speculation in the newspapers about a move. One report, two years previously, had suggested that Bayern Munich were wanting to sign him, but Anderson heard nothing. 'I would have considered an offer because Tony Woodcock was enjoying himself out there, but nobody approached me.' The following two years were not the happiest of Anderson's career. After lengthy talks with Clough, who handled all financial negotiations with his players, Anderson, at the age of twenty-six, signed a new two-year contract in the summer of 1982. In the absence of any firm alternative offer, there was no real reason to do otherwise. He had moved out of his parents' home in Clifton moving first to a house two miles away and then, with an eye to the future, to a large Victorian house on the outskirts of Nottingham. His family and his friends were in Nottingham. Only Forest's continued decline on the field could have caused him concern. In 1981–82 they had suffered their worst season since returning to the First Division, finishing twelfth and scoring a paltry forty-two goals. In the League Cup, they had been knocked out by Tottenham away, which was at least respectable; in the third round of the FA Cup, they had been convincingly beaten by Wrexham at home, which was rather less so. Wallace and Fashanu had been put on the transfer list at the end of the season and Peter Taylor had retired, only to join Derby County the following season.

'Viv was now one of the older players and so had to take on extra responsibilities on the pitch and in the dressing-room,' said Bowyer. 'If we were asked our opinion on whether we should stay overnight before a match, for example, Viv had a big say in it. A few years before, his opinion would have been swept under the carpet. In a sense, he had now come full circle.'

In his weekly column in the *Nottingham Evening Post* in December 1983, Anderson explained why he had decided to stay: 'I was content to play for Forest despite the fact that I'd seen a lot of faces disappear from our European Cup and Championship-winning teams. Not only that; being born and bred in Nottingham meant that my heart was in the city and that factor weighed heavily in favour of my staying rather than going on to accept a new challenge. So did the persuasive tongue of Brian Clough because with him at the helm you are always likely to win something.' But, he added significantly, 'after nearly ten years with the club, I don't know whether I'll be at Forest next season.' Unbeknown to him, Don Howe, coach at Arsenal, had made an approach to Clough in 1982 but Clough had stalled and the moment passed. Anderson only found out about it when he did finally join Don Howe at Arsenal in the summer of 1984.

In retrospect, Anderson now wishes he had left Forest in 1982 because, in effect, his career both at international and club level reached a plateau during the following two years. That was not entirely Forest's fault. In October 1982 Anderson badly twisted his right knee during an England training session for the match against West Germany, and as a result was out of the Forest side for nearly four months and out of the England team until April 1984. Forest were furious and in December, when it became clear that Anderson would be out for months rather than weeks, Clough demanded that the FA pay Anderson's £1000 a week salary.

When he returned to fitness, there were other problems. Forest had paid £30,000 for another full-back, Kenny Swain, from Aston Villa. Swain had initially been taken on loan by Clough as a short-term solution to Anderson's absence but had played so well that Clough had been persuaded to buy him. When Anderson came back, he was asked to play as a central defender. 'I refused and went to see Clough about it. For perhaps the only time during my career with Cloughie, I got my own way and Kenny moved to left-back.'

It was a sign of Anderson's growing personal strength and maturity – and perhaps his growing irritation – that he should confront Clough so squarely. Only a few years earlier he would not even have considered such effrontery. But this time the balance of power had shifted and Anderson was in a position of strength. Forest's resources were slender enough as it was without the loss of an international defender, and Clough knew as well as anyone that there would be no shortage of takers if his full-back asked for a transfer. Quite possibly, though, that little show of strength sealed Anderson's fate at the City Ground. Clough has never taken kindly to losing arguments with his players and though, by common consent, he had mellowed since the European Cup days, he was not likely to let it rest there. Sure enough, the following summer, he announced that Anderson and Wallace would have to accept a reduction in wages when their new contracts came up for renewal in the summer of 1984. Not surprisingly, neither was particularly struck with the idea. At the age of twenty-eight Anderson was looking to secure his future in the game, not to take his first look over the long path downhill.

All these little undercurrents of discontent which eddy around every club in the land did nothing to hinder a marked improvement by Forest on the field. In the 1982–83 season they finished fifth, qualifying for the UEFA Cup. Bill Shankly had dismissed the competition by saying that Liverpool 'had never finished low enough to qualify for it', but for Forest, after two seasons out of Europe, it was a financial lifeline. Forest reached the semi-final, knocking out Celtic on the way, and only an inspired performance by Anderlecht in the second leg when they won 3–0 to take the tie 3–2 on aggregate stopped an all-English final against Spurs. Unfortunately for Anderson, the Cup run proved the last straw in his growing disenchantment with both club and manager when, for once, Clough failed to keep a promise: bonuses which were promised were never paid.

Typically, there had been nothing in writing about the Forest players' bonuses for Europe. Forest were broke, the club would make little money from their first round match against an unknown East German club and, through club captain Ian Bowyer, Clough had asked that the players accept his word that he would 'see them right'. Bowyer was happy that anything promised to the players had been delivered in the past, and advised the team to accept Clough's word. Forest duly reached the semi-finals, playing lucrative ties against Celtic and Anderlecht, but the players never received their rewards.

'I was disappointed because in the past Clough had never let the players down,' said Anderson. 'I had never doubted his loyalty and, in a sense, that helped me make up my mind when Arsenal came in for me.' The transfer was as neat an affair as you are ever likely to find in the cloak-and-dagger world of football's slave market. True to form, negotiations took place in a motorway service station, but the move was so logical that there were few problems. Arsenal had been searching for a right-back since Pat Rice had retired several seasons before; Tony Woodcock had been signed from Cologne the previous season and was anxious to get his old Forest team-mate to Highbury; Don Howe, who had suceeded Terry Neill as Arsenal manger, already knew about Anderson from coaching the England squad; Forest, in their turn, had already indicated they could not afford Anderson's wages and there was a suspicion that Clough thought his full-back's best form had been left on the City Ground anyway, which was a strange judgement because the previous season had been Forest's best since 1978–79. They finished third in the championship as well as reaching the semi-final of the UEFA Cup. Anderson had more than played his part, playing forty games and, with the added duty of going up for set pieces, scoring six goals, including one in each of Forest's victories against Manchester United. In April he had been brought back into the England side for the match against Northern Ireland. Even by his own admission, he was actually playing better than when he made his debut for England. 'At that time I was happy enough with my form, but every run of matches was littered with below-par performances. This season I've achieved a higher level of consistency. I wouldn't say I've been turning in breathtaking stuff every week, but I don't think I've had a really bad match all season,' said Anderson at the time.

'I think Brian Clough thought Viv had come to the end of his First Division career,' said Don Howe. 'One or two people I've spoken to said that Brian put it around that we'd bought a pup, but, actually, the boy improved.

'I'd obviously noticed Viv first in our games against Forest and had always admired him. I suppose that because he was tall and black – at a time when there were not so many coloured players around – he did stand out. But he also had this enormous stride. He seemed to get from one penalty-area to the other in about five strides. He was a very striking player, very quick. A player like that hits you between the eyes. When I joined the England set-up with Ron Greenwood in 1981, I got to know him better and found out he had a terrific personality too.

'We'd had a problem with the right full-back spot at Arsenal and tried several different players without finding a replacement for Pat Rice, and I'd made enquiries about Viv in 1981. I think if we'd paid over the odds for him, say £500,000, we might have got him, but Clough never said yes and he never said no.'

In 1984, when Arsenal made another offer of £275,000, Anderson needed little persuasion. The thought of leaving his friends, his family and his home town nagged at the back of his mind, but ambition and curiosity, quite apart from financial incentives, quickly outweighed his natural conservatism. Besides, he was not alone now in making decisions. In June 1984, in one of the bolder and more impromptu moments in his life, Anderson got married – without telling his parents or his friends. The only people at the wedding were the photographer and his brother, who acted as witnesses, and the registrar of West Bridgford.

Viv's bride was Debra Tassi, a girl from the same Clifton Estate. He had met her a few years before in the unlikely surroundings of the local tennis club, and, soon after, she went out in the Forest party to the European Cup final against Hamburg. At the time, her knowledge of football was so scant that she did not realize that Hamburg's equalizer had been disallowed or that Forest had won the Cup. Since then, she has become Anderson's number one fan and critic, a dual role she plays with some skill. Marriage had been in the air for over a year, but the possibility of a move to London in the summer of 1984 made a decision more urgent.

'It just seemed right,' said Debra. 'We sat down and thought about who should come and who should sit where, until Viv said: "No, I can't do with this," and so we decided to just go and do it. At the wedding, Viv had beads of sweat on his forehead. He wanted to get it over with as quickly as possible. In the afternoon, he went to watch the cricket and I stayed at home and ate the cake.'

EIGHT

# THE MODEL PRO

Professional football is a strange, precious, neurotic, insular, hothouse world. Players scan the papers in the morning not just to find out what sex and scandal has been revealed in which dressing-room, but to check that their job is still safe. Imagine, for example, how Arsenal's Kenny Sansom must have felt when he discovered that his manager had just paid £400,000 for Nigel Winterburn, another left full-back, five years younger, or how John Sivebaek received the news that Alex Ferguson had bought Anderson, an England international, for £250,000 in the summer of 1987. Security? Football does not know the meaning of the word. For, quite apart from the constant reminder that the body is not unbreakable, that a career can be ended any day in the most innocuous of tackles, footballers' lives are manipulated by a whole host of forces, over which they have as much control as a puppet. Manager, chairman, board, press – all, in their various ways, have more influence over a player's fate than the player himself.

In the current climate, where success is whispered on every prevailing wind, the pace of change has quickened appreciably. A manager has only to lose three games in a row and he is faced with a crisis or with the readers of some national newspaper being polled on whether he should keep his job or not. A player has only to be dropped once for his future at the club to be in doubt, for exclusive headlines to reveal that he is the target for Pisa, Sampdoria, Senegal Rovers or some club he probably has not heard of. In the midst of the storm, the player himself has to find his own firm ground, and just as it would be wrong to portray the modern professional footballer as the innocent victim of evil forces so it would be equally wrong to brand him a money-grabbing mercenary who would sell his soul to the devil – or at least the *Sun* – for the price of a reserve full-back.

A top-class footballer makes good money. Anderson himself, if he fulfils his four-year contract at Manchester United, could earn over £400,000. In addition there is the odd promotional extra organized through his company Anderson Promotions and a three-year contract with Puma worth less than £10,000. He will also get a loyalty bonus each year he stays with United. A few years ago, such bonuses were in theory impromptu *ex gratia* payments by a club, in practice usually tied up in complicated negotiations over transfer fees, in which 'you scratch my back, I'll scratch yours' was the one moral guideline. So, instead of a fee being set at £250,000, it became £275,000, the extra going into the player's pocket. Partly because of the increased sophistication of the taxman, partly because of the increased financial acumen of the average footballer, such practices have largely died out. The age of the agent has given way to the age of the accountant.

'Players are more cautious now than they were when I started in the game,' Anderson said. 'They are also more clued up. Not long ago, it was a case of get it, spend it, but now players are thinking about pensions and looking ahead more. They view the game more as a business. Most have accountants; I think you'd be hard pushed to find five agents working in the game now. They never used to do much anyway and they were still taking their 18 per cent or whatever and most of the work they got you I could have got for myself anyway.'

Anderson is the first to admit that he has done well out of the game but he has prepared himself well against the slings and arrows of football's outrageous fortunes. He automatically pays a certain percentage of his weekly wage into the Professional Footballers' Association fund for when he retires, but also has his own pension fund which he can use when he reaches the ripe old age of thirty-five. He has a house in Hertfordshire, a flat in Manchester and a big black Mercedes with a personalized number plate. Life is sweet. But suggest that it has not been earned by good honest sweat and you will get an uncharacteristically sharp response.

'I've earned the right to be paid well. I began on £8 a week as an apprentice and won a League Championship medal on £80 a week. I've learnt my trade and come through the ranks just like anyone else and it's only been at Arsenal and at Manchester United that I've started to cash in on the hard work I've put into the game. There is not as much money in football as people think. I'm not complaining because I've had a better career than most, but I don't feel guilty about the money I get. It's a short career and you have to make good while you can.'

One of the least profitable sections of Anderson's well organized financial operation is playing for his country. If he was a real business company, he would have sold off that division long ago. Remarkably, his share of the marketing pool privately organized by the players came to just £6000 and was paid two years after the event.

From the World Cup in 1982 Anderson earned £9000 gross, a good sum if you happen to be out of work in Tyneside, peanuts when compared to the six-figure amounts reputedly pocketed by the winning Italian team. In 1986, he was paid (promptly) £20,000 for the World Cup. When he gets selected for England, Anderson is paid £325-a-match set fee with a bonus if the team qualifies for the World Cup or the European Championships, and £10 a day pocket money. But he gets no fee from the television rights and the match fee covers all the days taken for training and travelling. Test cricketers are paid over £1500 for a five-day match and though the international footballer is only performing for ninety minutes, he is with the squad for a minimum of four days, so the comparison is not unreasonable. Rightly, perhaps, there is still a notion of honour and patriotism included in the financial bargaining.

There is no doubt that a player now has far more of a say over his own financial future than he used to. He no longer has to pay a compulsory five per cent of his signing-on fee to the Football League, and can negotiate his own wages and his own signing-on fee, a task carried out in negotiations with Manchester United by Anderson's accountant, Alan Baines. But, on the other side of the coin, Anderson is adamant that a player also has a duty to stick by the terms of the contract he has negotiated and signed. 'I was slaughtered by one article in the *Daily Mirror*, when I left Arsenal, for being disloyal to the club that had done me so well. That really annoyed me. I had fulfilled every letter of my contract with the club, I had done my three years and never let them down. So when my contract was up I was free to look at other offers if I wanted to. It's up to the individual to negotiate the best deal he possibly can, but once he has done that he can't go back after a year and start complaining because someone else is earning more. You should serve the time of your contract and then go in for more. The player can't have it both ways.'

For some reason, perhaps not entirely divorced from the increasingly litigious sporting age in which we live, I had imagined a player's contract to be a huge wordy document full of heretofores and hereinafters. In fact, it is as brief and as omnipotent as the Ten Commandments. 'The Player hereby agrees to play in an efficient manner and to the best of his ability for the Club for the period . . . The Player shall not engage in any business or live in any place which the Directors (or Committee) of the Club may deem unsuitable ... The Player shall not directly or indirectly induce a Player employed by another Club to leave that employment for any purpose or reason whatsoever ...' And so on. But the real catch-all condition of the contract is the following: 'The Player shall do everything necessary to get and keep himself in the best possible condition so as to render the most efficient service to the Club ...' In effect, that means that a player's whole life must be conducted with one end in view, to play like a wizard every Saturday afternoon. Commandments, of course, can be ignored as easily as obeyed, and plenty of players do the former. They do not include Anderson nor, equally importantly, his wife.

'Sometime friends ring up for Viv and I say: "He's out at work" and they'll laugh and say "Oh, he's got a proper job now has he." That really gets us annoyed,' said Debra. 'People think footballers have a really easy life – train once a day, play once or twice a week and have a good time for the rest of the week. But actually our lives are more stressful than most because of the routine and the insecurity. You don't know what's going to happen from one day to the next. Viv could be dropped or injured tomorrow.

'It's a weird life. Twenty-four hours of every single day for the last five years has been concentrated on getting Viv playing well on a Saturday afternoon. On a Friday night if something has upset me and I want to have a blazing row about it, I won't because I think it will upset him. It's like you are running your own business. Viv is the business, but I'm part of the business too, and though I don't go to work myself I often feel if Viv has a bad game that it's partly my fault. It's ridiculous.'

For the amateur, who goes out to play his Sunday morning game for fun and not money, this is the hidden world of professionalism. He can imitate the professional quite easily – shouting at the referee, upending the centre-forward when he's clean through and then justifying it on semi-professional grounds – but he can never understand the frustrations and the forces that go into ninety minutes on a Saturday afternoon. But then he's not getting paid £2000 a week, either.

Debra goes on: 'My whole life is dominated by the weekly cycle. If you're doing well then it's great, but you can go from the heights to the depths in one week. When we were knocked out of the League Cup by Oxford United it was terrible. It was embarrassing more than anything, because friends kept ringing up and saying: "I thought you'd win that one." It's not just the money, it's your pride.

'Sometimes I envy the fans who can watch it just as a game, win or lose. You don't watch it as a game, you watch it as everything. When Viv comes home after the team's lost, I try to tell him it's not everything and to put the whole thing into perspective by telling him how much better off he is than most. But I don't think he really believes it. The game's our living.'

The intensity of Anderson's commitment to his profession seems out of keeping with his manner. In general, he has a take-it-or-leave-it attitude which makes his claim that he would have been happy as a printer wholly believable. But, whether because of Clough's early discipline, a fiercely competitive nature (which extends to upsetting the Scrabble board if he is losing), or the fear that he might lose all that he has built up, the casualness stops well this side of work. Football is serious, and though he is intelligent enough to know that 'kicking a bag of wind about', as he says, is not the meaning of life, it just happens to be the meaning of his life at the moment. So when he has a bad game, when he does not live up to the high standards he has come to expect of himself, the kindness and the charm can turn to moodiness, the natural ebullience to introversion. Off the field he is invariably polite and gentle to outsiders, loud and cheerful to his team-mates; on the field he even surprises his wife by his aggression, which is vented in equal measure on the referee and the opposing winger.

'Away from football there's not an ounce of aggression in him,' said Debra. 'Even if someone had me in a headlock, he'd probably just tap him on the shoulder and ask him politely if he'd let go. In a game, he's completely different. His moodiness comes out as aggression and it looks awful sometimes. At Arsenal, it got ridiculous at one point because he was getting booked every week. Apart from anything, it was costing us money because he got fined by the club every time he was booked.'

Off the field Anderson admits that he couldn't kick his granny. On the field, he is the epitome of the professional. His moral guidelines are laid down quite simply. If the ref spots it, it's wrong; everything else (apart from deliberately trying to injure an opponent – 'I'll kick someone but I won't deliberately try to hurt them') is all right. Maradona's handballed goal which knocked England out of the World Cup was, by that logic, totally without stain or blame.

'If someone is through and likely to score, then I will definitely upend him. That's part and parcel of the game. I'd do that without thinking. I'd commit a professional foul, if need be, if it was the right thing at the right time. The alternative is him going round me, putting the ball in the net and us losing 1–0. If it means me getting sent off – and it's probably right that I should be – and the team getting something from the game, that is better than us getting nothing. Nine times out of ten I think I can get the ball in a tackle anyway, but the tenth time, by hook or by crook, I've got to try and stop him. Probably my views are wrong, but I'm a professional and I can't let somebody just run through and put the ball in the net without me trying to do something about it. If it was cricket, I'd wait until somebody told me I was out. Walking? You must be joking. I can't understand anyone doing that.

'You would probably say that I was a cheat, but I'd just say I'm a professional trying to win a game on a Saturday afternoon. Whether that means handballing accidentally-on-purpose to score, or upending someone, I'd do it and it's up to the referee to spot it and penalize it.'

Logically, the other side of the coin should be a stoically professional acceptance of the referee's decision if it goes against him. Anderson does not quite see it that way, though he has the good grace to accept the illogicality. 'I know I am advocating tactics designed to dupe the referee and make him get his decisions wrong. But, of course, I go bananas if the ref gets it wrong against us.' In a sense, the code of conduct on the professional football field does follow a crazy logic. At least everybody knows where they stand. In cricket, after the events on England's tour of Pakistan in late 1987, there is no such certainty. Cricketers and the authorities are torn between the notion of 'playing the game' and recognizing that the days when players could be relied upon to do the decent thing have long since passed, at least in international cricket. Football crossed that barrier fifty years ago and so there is no hypocrisy. The main problem for the footballer is the standard of refereeing, which in Anderson's opinion has deteriorated markedly over the past few seasons. 'They are so inconsistent. One week you will get a really good one, and the next three will be awful. I don't know their names, but I know their faces and which ones are decent.'

At the age of thirty-two, Anderson is at the time of life when he should, by rights, have learnt that physical aggression is a waste of both time and precious energy. The truth is somewhat different. 'I'm getting worse. When you are young and somebody kicks you, you just accept it and get on with it, but when you get older it hurts more.'

Anderson sees a game of football very much as a personal and psychological battle with his winger. He had a long-standing joke with Tony Woodcock at Forest, and later at Arsenal, that if the opposition had a particularly fast and tricky winger, Anderson would say: 'Yes, but he can't play without legs.' It was only half a joke, no joke at all if you happened to be on the receiving end of one of Anderson's early tackles, which he refers to with a grin as 'just saying hello'. It was once said by a wizened old professional batsman that 'you can't trust bowlers, you never know what they're going to do next'. Anderson has much the same view of wingers.

'You are trying to establish a physical dominance over an opponent, particularly as a full-back. I didn't think about it so much earlier in my career because I did not need to, but now I'm a bit older and people start taking liberties, so I think: 'Well, I'm not standing for this, I think I'll get one in first.' Just so that he knows it's not going to be an easy afternoon for him and that anything he gets he is going to have to work for. It might be cynical, but that's football.

'I like to get a strong tackle in early in the game, just to leave my mark. But, after that, giving away stupid fouls in stupid areas can cost you goals. The best place is either side of the halfway line because if it's a free-kick they're not going to score from there, are they? Fouling is part of the game because football is a physical game, but my disciplinary record is pretty good considering how long I've played.'

In his game, just as much as in his character, Anderson is a strange mixture. In stature, he is not the typical full-back. Full-backs should be built like George Cohen, small and square with a low centre of gravity and as solid as a brick wall. Anderson is six foot one, eleven and a half stone, with legs so prominent that all his nicknames are variations on the same theme: 'The Extension', 'Spiderman', 'The Spider'. By common consent, he is not the world's most ferocious tackler; even Don Howe, who is Anderson's number one fan, admits that. 'If he has a fault, it's his striking for the ball in a tackle. He gets his timing wrong and he can get a bit emotional in a game if things aren't going right. He's a runner rather than a tackler. He's very good at guiding a winger to where he wants to go and then nicking the ball off him rather than winning the ball in a one-on-one tackle.'

Anderson's own first rule of full-back play reflects that. 'Stay on your feet the whole time. If you dive in on a winger, you are making up his mind for him and you don't want to do that. If you are standing there in front of him, he's got to get round you and to do that consistently is very difficult. You can't do anything when you're flat on your back. The sliding tackle should only be used as the last resort. Ideally, you want to get to the winger at the same time as he gets the ball so that he has no time to settle or build up momentum. The last thing you want is for the winger to be attacking you with ten yards of space in front so that he has time to build up speed. If that happens, you want to know where your right midfield player is because it's really his job to stop the winger from doing that. If he does run at you, then I try to jockey him, push him or whatever into the area I want him to go. In general, if he is going to cross the ball then you want him to do it from far out so that your central defenders are heading the ball further away from goal. You don't want him crossing from the by-line. I know I'm not a crunching tackler, but I've had to adapt my game to suit my long legs. Sometimes it's an advantage, sometimes it's not.'

Anderson's emergence as one of the best full-backs in the country coincided with changing notions of how the game shoud be played. The brilliant Dutch side of the early 1970s had shown that skill and athleticism did not have to be the preserve of forwards and midfield players. Total Football, as it was grandly called, simply meant that everyone in the team should be able to play, a theory the South Americans had absorbed thirty years previously. So full-backs like Anderson and David Nish who were quick and knew what to do with the ball when they got it – 'cultured', as the tabloids liked to call them – were very much the fashion.

As Martin O'Neill puts it, 'You have to be a nice footballer to play full-back now. Clough spent £250,000 on Nish, which was unheard of for a full-back in those days, because he was a lovely footballer. There has been a levelling-out of positions since the mid 1970s when the centre-half had to be able to head the ball, a sweeper played alongside him who was small and quick and full-backs whose first job was to get forward. At the time Viv started there were a lot of wingers playing brilliantly at full-back. Terry Cooper was perhaps the first who really played like a winger. But there were only about four or five real wingers in the game so Viv's game was based on picking up something loose, striding forward and looking impressive.' The Irishman has a healthy disdain for the art of the full-back. 'It's the easiest position on the field. It's a doddle. If I could come back now, I'd come back as a full-back, kick the winger to death, never get roasted, come forward now and again and play 1,000 games.'

Anderson, not surprisingly, does not quite see it that way. 'Defending is an art, just like any other part of the game. Clough appreciated it, so did George Graham at Arsenal. We spent hours working on defensive techniques at Arsenal – one-on-one, four-on-one – just seeing how you coped, and practising jockeying and tackling. Though defending is a team job, not just the job of any individual, defenders have to be able to defend as individuals and together as a unit. One player can have a brilliant game but you'll still lose 4–0 if everybody else isn't doing their job as well.

'Full-back is as much a specialist position as anywhere else and in the last ten years full-backs are being asked to do a lot more. You're expected to create by going forward and getting good crosses in, to defend and to score a few goals. You have to be good at all three.'

For England goalkeeper Peter Shilton, height, heading ability and reliability were Anderson's greatest assets. The relationship between a goalkeeper and his full-back is a delicate and volatile one. More than any other pairing on the field, they rely on each other for their living. Mistakes can cost goals and jobs. In particular, Shilton appreciated Anderson's reliability on the far post where goalkeepers often fear to tread. 'Headers from the far post or people coming round the back – goalkeepers can't do much about those things, but if you have a good reliable full-back you can work around them. You can position yourself easier when you know what the full-back is going to do and you know when you're not playing with a good one because he's never there when you need him. Viv was always there,' said Shilton.

Shilton was never quite so happy with Anderson's positional play in the early days, but admits that often he was deceived by his pace and by his reach. 'I used to have a go at him for not tucking in more behind the centre-halves to cover and then the ball would come through and I'm thinking he's not going to make it, but, sure enough, he would come flying across and his long legs would go in and take the ball away.' Tony Woodcock recalls being the victim of Anderson's famous Extension too. 'He was uncanny. You'd just think you'd got past him and this long leg would come out and the ball was gone. With his legs and his elbows, which were lethal, you had a helluva job trying to get past him in one piece.'

Ironically, if there is a weakness in his game now it's a tendency to over-cover. Anderson is aware of the criticism. 'Gordon Strachan tells me about it – marking the centre-forward rather than the winger, but that's what Clough drilled into me and it's the way I've been taught. Perhaps it's because I'm a bit cocksure of myself. I know if the ball goes over my head I have the pace to get out there, and in the penalty-area I'd rather be defending the immediate danger in the middle, particularly around the penalty-spot, because if it goes to the far post I've always got a chance to get across and block. That's just the way I play.'

Whatever the technical qualities of his game, the quality that the Manchester United manager Alex Ferguson noted during a thoroughly ill-tempered game against Arsenal in the 1986–87 season was his aggression. Ferguson was so impressed by the abuse that he was given throughout the second half by Anderson that he resolved to bring him to Old Trafford. That sort of enthusiasm and aggression from a thirty-year-old, he reasoned, must be worth having in his side. Anderson himself puts that down to an overwhelming desire to win, be it snooker, Scrabble, golf or Trivial Pursuits.

But the key to the Anderson psyche, if there is one, is that he is totally and head-over-heels in love with the game of football. He admits that if he won £1 million tomorrow he would still go on playing. Every morning, rain or shine, he bounces out of bed to go to work. Never once has his wife heard him moan about it, not even during pre-season training when life for everyone within groaning distance of a professional footballer becomes unbearable. Anderson dislikes training, or to be more precise he dislikes the running involved in the training. He'll play football all day, but running just for the sake of keeping fit has never been his strength. On his first training session at Arsenal, the players were sent out on a five-mile run. Anderson was crawling along at the back when he heard footsteps and puffing behind him. 'It was Don Howe. He'd started the run late but was about to overtake me.'

However, there are no shortage of character references for Anderson, which is one of the reasons he has enjoyed such an extraordinarily long and successful career. Managers like good footballers, but they also like players who are genuine and enthusiastic. In short, players who will give them no trouble. Don Howe, for example, puts Anderson alongside Bryan Robson, Ray Wilkins and Peter Reid in his category of 'super blokes'.

'I never had any worries about him at Arsenal. He was always bouncy, he loved his work, he was great for team spirit because he was always on the end of any practical jokes flying around, and he never looked for excuses. A lot of players do, you know. Everything is wrong with everybody else, but they don't look at themselves. Tony

Woodcock was a bit like that, but Viv wanted to put things right if he thought they were going wrong. I would hold him up to anyone as an example. In retrospect, I might have made him captain of the club because he would have made a good one.'

'Viv was no problem to anybody,' said Martin O'Neill. 'He was just happy to be playing football. Normally when you call someone a model professional, it's a load of rubbish. But, in Viv's case, it's true.'

NINE

# METHOD AND MEDIOCRITY

*Oh, London is a fine town,*
*A very famous city,*
*Where all the streets are paved with gold,*
*And all the maidens pretty.*

The offer of a transfer to Arsenal in 1984 could not have come at a better time for Anderson. After ten years at Forest, he was beginning to find life stale, success increasingly elusive. He knew all of Clough's phrases off by heart, and though still a little overawed by the man he was no longer responding so well to his particular brand of motivation. With so little money to play with, Clough had less room to manoeuvre and his underlying threat to sell a player, international or not, if he didn't perform to standard carried less weight when the team was not winning. However, Anderson hardly left a sinking ship. Forest finished third in the league in the season before he left, which was still a division and a half above where he joined them in 1974. No one, not even Clough, could begrudge Anderson a move to a more prestigious and progressive club. In his weekly column in the local paper Clough wrote: 'As I see it, Viv left our club simply because he wanted a change after ten years at the City Ground. And who can blame him? I certainly can't . . . He gave Forest such magnificent service there is no way we should ever complain about his decision to head south.'

Clough hasn't said a word to him since, but at least Anderson seemed to go with the understanding if not the blessing of the man who had made him. At the time, Anderson made noises about 'regretting it for the rest of his life if he didn't take the chance' (he said exactly the same later about moving to Manchester United), which makes him out to be far more passive in the decision than he was. Only a few years previously, the prospect of leaving his home town, his friends and family would not have entered his head for a moment. But being one of the senior professionals at Forest, being back in the England side and, above all, being married gave him the confidence to tackle the big city. Besides, the money was better.

'I'd always said that I couldn't play in London because we had such a tight-knit community at Forest. But when it came, I wished it had come a bit earlier. I suppose everyone asks themselves, "Can I go and play for a big club?" It's not that I was uncertain about my own ability, but at a big club in a big city there are a lot of distractions and I wondered if I could cope with them.'

Debra had uncertainties, too. 'It was quite frightening at first because it was so different – the people, the place. If we'd stayed in Nottingham, we would not have got the same range of experience.' While Anderson fitted into the Arsenal side remarkably easily, socially the transformation was a bit more difficult. 'I remember we went to a dinner for Cancer Research not long after we'd come to the club,' Debra recalled. 'All the other guests seemed to be from Oxford or Cambridge. They spoke beautifully and there we were with our Nottingham accents. My immediate reaction was "Oh help, I wish we'd never come." But two people came across to talk to us and we began to talk about Salvadore Dali. Luckily, a friend has a Dali lithograph and only a few days before I'd asked her about it, so I knew a little about him. Viv was absolutely flabbergasted. "How did you know about Salvadore Dali?" he asked. I could have walked out after two minutes, but we stayed and had a fantastic evening.'

Anderson had been impressed by Don Howe's ambition. He knew and respected Howe from the England squad and he had experienced the Midlander's deep passion for the game. Howe, for his part, had seen the Arsenal double side take shape and, now that he had inherited the manager's job from Terry Neill, he was able to shape a side in his own image. Above all, like Anderson, he wanted to relive success. Tony Woodcock and Charlie Nicholas had been brought to the club to join stalwarts like David O'Leary and Kenny Sansom, talented young players like Paul Davis. With Anderson filling the right-back spot and the incomparable Pat Jennings in goal, the defence, at least, seemed watertight. Arsenal, it was whispered through the streets of North London, were ready to win the title again. It never happened. Every season they threatened, every season they faded.

'When Viv came to Arsenal the club was changing,' explained Howe. 'We had Charlie and Tony Woodcock and we were trying to find the right blend. But it wasn't working out exactly as I wanted. It was a bit hit-and-miss. One week we went to Villa and won 6–0, the next we lost 1–0 at home. Viv was part of it all and it must have been very frustrating for him because he was providing some very solid work. Week in week out he was one of our best players and I think he became a better, more confident player at Arsenal than he was in his last years at Forest. He certainly won back his England place, which was no more than he deserved.'

If Howe was impressed with the confidence and maturity of his purchase from Nottingham, Anderson was impressed by the size and prestige of the club. Highbury, with its statues and marble halls, its huge corridors and its tradition, was so far removed from the provincial cosiness of the City Ground that it seemed like a different world. Everything was on a bigger scale – the training ground, the pay cheques, victory, defeat. 'Football in London is big business,' said Anderson. 'At Forest, we played good football and a lot of our games were very entertaining, win or lose. But there was not that much expected of you even after we'd won the League Championship and the European Cup. We were still a footballing backwater compared to Arsenal, which is why it can be very difficult coming down from the north to play in London. A lot more is expected of you. I mean, if you lost a game at home it was devastating – the newspapers, the punters, everyone was doom and gloom. At Forest, we weren't expected to beat Manchester United, so there was no pressure on us to do so.

'We were very much in the shadow of the double-winning side at Arsenal. When we had an unbeaten run of seventeen league games we were forever reading that Bertie Mee said we were not as good as the double-winning side. It became boring in the end, but clubs have different traditions. At Arsenal, we were always tagged 'boring' no matter how we played and maybe we did try to stop other sides from playing first before trying to create something ourselves. At Manchester United, the tradition stems from Charlton and Best. You let the other side play and then play better. Perhaps that's why we've not won the championship in the last twenty years. Sometimes you have to scrap very hard to win points. I think Alex Ferguson appreciates that – I only hope the crowd will as well.'

When he moved to Old Trafford in the summer of 1987, Anderson came to understand that Highbury was not quite the Everest he had imagined, but it must have seemed like it when he arrived in 1984. But, apart from living in a hotel for nine months, constantly having to travel back up the motorway to Nottingham and searching endlessly for a house – none of which, he says, was conducive to preparing for a football match – Anderson relished the challenge.

He quickly impressed manager and supporters with his consistency and dedication. After doing things the Clough way for ten years, any other way was bound to be a shock – Arsenal used to do terrible things like train, hard. No gentle walks through the park or half-hour five-a-sides; it was running and weights and a weekly visit to the scales. 'I asked Tony Woodcock about how hard the training was before I decided to move and he said, "Not too bad." After the first few days, I was nearly dead and I gave Woodie a terrible time.'

Anderson, at least, had some experience of life outside Clough from playing for England under Ron Greenwood, and it stood him in good stead in his early days at Highbury. 'I knew that we trained differently from Forest,' said Howe. 'Cloughie has different methods – no coaching and lots of time off. I'm not knocking that because it's brought him tremendous success, but I'm a coach and I do things differently. Being with England helped Viv because Ron Greenwood was a coach, so Viv accepted the change. In fact, he settled down so easily at Arsenal that after three months people thought he'd been at the club for years. That's all credit to Viv because he trained very well. He says he hates it, but I'm not sure because there was no day when I thought he didn't fancy it. I certainly never had to get on to him about putting in more effort.'

Anderson consciously resisted the temptation to compare notes from past days of glory, though in quieter moments he and Woodcock would doubtless have bemoaned the amount of training. At Forest, all they had to do was play the game simply inside a rigid team framework. Pass the ball to a red shirt, play it to feet, hold on to the ball, support the man on the ball, get it wide, sling in a cross, goal. Easy. And the game was so stripped down, so unpretentious, it didn't matter what the opposition did because, nine times out of ten, whatever they did wasn't good enough anyway. At Arsenal, they couldn't afford to be so simple. As Don Howe said: 'If my team is winning, I can be out playing golf every afternoon or down at the supermarket with the wife and no one will say a thing. But if my team are not winning, then I've got a problem and I have to be seen to be doing something about it.' With Clough, it didn't matter a damn. In the end, he was bigger than the club so within limits, win, lose or draw, he could do what he liked. At Highbury, there was no such freedom, not for the manager, not for the coach, not for the players. Every little detail had to be right and, more important, to be seen to be right.

While Clough reckoned that other sides should worry about his side, Howe's assistant Wilf Dixon prepared detailed dossiers on the opposition, which were delivered to the team each Friday. On one occasion, recorded by Tony Woodcock in his book *Inside Soccer*, Dixon agonized over whether one of the opposition midfield players was five foot six tall or five foot seven. The Dixon rundowns became a standing joke among the team and were total anathema to the former Forest players, but, in general, Anderson found that the structure of the Arsenal side was not unlike that of Forest. Brian Talbot wide on the right like Martin O'Neill, Graham Rix wide on the left like John Robertson, two strong central defenders like Burns and Lloyd, and Woodcock, well, like Woodcock. The only problem was that Arsenal tried to make the game more complicated than it really was. To an extent, that was Howe's fault.

'Don is a great student of the game and goes to watch lots of matches. So we used to try lots of different things and different systems. The problem was that sometimes we were not quite sure which way we were going to play from one week to the next,' said Anderson. For a time, Arsenal even adopted the Watford way, hitting long balls into space, eschewing any pretty-pretty build-up in midfield and knocking it up to the centre-forwards as far up the field as possible. Under the knowledgeable and respected eye of John Cartwright, who had been brought in as assistant manager by Don Howe, the Arsenal players attempted to put the theory into practice during the 1985-86 season. Apart from reaching the quarter-final of the Milk Cup, where they were knocked out by Aston Villa, the method was not a success. 'A lot of us didn't like it. It just wasn't Arsenal's game but John had seen other people get success that way and wanted us to try it, and so we went along with it. The players, though, weren't too happy about it – Steve Williams didn't like it for one, and told Howe so. So he was dropped.'

After two seasons of mediocrity, Howe bowed out with characteristic dignity. He is happier as a coach, out on the training-ground teaching players the game, than he is sitting behind a desk managing. He is also too nice a man. His successor was George Graham, a member of the double-winning side, whose gentle skills on the field belied his toughness off it. Graham had a Clough-style sense of discipline and more than once in the press Anderson likened the new Arsenal manage-r to Clough. 'I've not crossed him yet, but I wouldn't like to,' he said at the time. 'I think there might be an explosion. You ask me what I think of the new manager, I'll tell you after we've lost three games in a row.'

In Graham's first full season at Highbury, 1986-87, which was also the last of Anderson's three-year contract, it did look for a moment as if Arsenal would finally fulfil expectations and win the league. With a side built on the youth of David Rocastle, Tony Adams, Niall Quinn, Martin Hayes and Perry Groves, they put together a run of seventeen league matches without defeat, including thirteen victories. From the middle of November to the end of January, they were top of the league. As ever, their success was based on a rigid defensive technique that from the beginning of September to the end of January conceded just seven goals in nineteen league games. It was defence *à la* Forest, a stifling blanket designed to snuff out any signs of a fire in the opposition's midfield. Surprisingly, too, it was constructed by a man whose delicate skills as a player were always dedicated to undoing such rigidity.

'Graham spent a lot of time on organizing the defence and it paid off. But, to begin with, I used to argue with him a lot about the way he wanted us to play,' Anderson recalled. At Forest, Anderson had always guided his winger down the line, encouraging him the whole time to run away from goal, safe in the knowledge that with his pace and his long legs, the winger would rarely be able to get a decent cross in. As long as the individual did his job, there was no danger. Graham did not like to take that chance. He wanted – ordered would be a better word – his full-backs to guide the winger into the middle, back into the ruck of players, thereby suffocating the move at birth. The system was designed to stop the opposing players from reaching the by-line and pulling back a cross.

'At Forest, we played more in a line in the back four, and if we played offside then the full-backs played them because they were last in the line and could see all the way along the line. At United we defend much further back than at Arsenal anyway, and we very rarely play offside. At Arsenal, the full-backs played in front of the two centre-halves and the golden rule was that if our midfield was putting pressure on the player with the ball, we pushed out because there was not a lot he could do. If he was not under pressure and had plenty of time, then you stayed in position because if you pushed out, you became very vulnerable. He could put the ball into space behind you and do loads of things. Nine times out of ten, if you put pressure on the ball then you could catch them offside. It was risky but if you practised, it worked well,' Anderson explained. It might not have been pretty, but it was mighty effective. Still very much an individual at heart, Anderson took time to adapt to this team pattern. He argued at first, then accepted that it worked, although, if you pushed him, he would still prefer to play the way he did at Forest.

As he was constantly reminded by both Sansom and O'Leary, Anderson, at the age of thirty, was the oldest member of that Arsenal side. He was also the most experienced – at least in terms of winning medals – and knew what it took to win the league. Arsenal, he felt, were too young to keep up the momentum, though he gained no satisfaction from being proved right. 'With kids, sooner or later you're going to reach your level. We were as surprised as anyone that we kept it going as long as we did because it took a lot out of them physically and mentally. Realistically, I didn't think we could win the league, and I said so at the time.'

Sure enough, the Arsenal challenge blew up in a big way. After losing at Manchester United and having David Rocastle sent off (Anderson very nearly followed him for a prolonged assault on the limbs of Whiteside and the eardrums of the referee), Arsenal lost five, drew three of the next eight games and dropped to fourth in the league. They scored one goal in nine games and not even a defence of Arsenal's calibre could cope with that sort of drought. But there was consolation in the Littlewoods Cup as Arsenal made their way to Wembley in the sweetest possible way, with a protracted semi-final victory over their deadly rivals Spurs. Anderson began his side's revival with a toe-poked equalizer in the second leg when it looked as though Arsenal were on the way out. It might not have been a classic strike, but the fact that he was in the penalty-area at all was a relatively new development in Anderson's game. In his final year at Forest, he had scored six goals, but before that he had rarely been required to go up for set pieces. He is not a thumping header of the ball, in the mould of Burns, but his height and reach can cause considerable unrest at corners and free-kicks and, during his final year at Highbury, he scored seven goals, which is a fair strike-rate for a full-back.

The final at Wembley against Liverpool was to provide the one footballing highlight in Anderson's three years at Highbury, and his first medal for seven years. Even that was won the hard way as Liverpool took the lead through the inevitable Rush. Liverpool, you remember, had never lost when Rush had scored, and only one person in the whole stadium voiced the opinion that the sequence was about to end. The lone voice was Anderson's wife Debra.

'When Rush scored, I remember saying to Joy O'Leary that I thought we would win. It was mainly because I knew Viv would commit suicide if we lost. Some players don't seem to take it so seriously,' she said later.

The fact that the two winning goals were scored by Charlie Nicholas added an extra piquancy to the victory. It was no secret that Nicholas was not exactly George Graham's flavour of the month, but his goals brought at least a temporary truce. Since arriving at Highbury in June 1983, Nicholas had been infuriatingly inconsistent, never reproducing the form which had delighted the crowds at Parkhead. He was a manager's nightmare: bags of talent, but little sign of it on Saturday afternoons. Yet, on the terraces, in the newspapers and in the dressing-room, Nicholas, with his casual wit and his natural ebullience, was a thoroughly popular character. As the only man in the Highbury dressing-room louder than Anderson himself, the pair became firm friends. The friendship was based on a common ability to enjoy life, but also on strong mutual respect. Anderson has always wanted to be the skilful, flashy centre-forward, scoring brilliant goals and nonchalantly accepting the idolatry of the fans – 'inside this full-back's body there is a centre-forward dying to get out' – and Nicholas admired Anderson's stability and discipline. He also needed his caution and suspicion.

'Charlie had tremendous ability, but he would be the first to admit that he has never produced it consistently, for whatever reason – pressure, lifestyle. He admits now that he should never have done all the modelling photos he did when he first arrived at the club. That gave him a 'Champagne Charlie' image which stayed with him and was often given as the reason why he did not perform consistently. We used to talk about his game a bit, but he's such a nice lad that if I'd have known what was wrong I would have told him. Perhaps it was the combination of being at a club that was too big for him, of the system we played, I don't know. He always moaned that we didn't play the ball to his feet, that he was always having to chase it, which wasn't his game. But he'll do really well at a club if he finds that little bit of consistency,' said Anderson.

But football is a kaleidoscopic world; nothing remains the same for long. No sooner had the Littlewoods success been banked than life took an entirely unexpected turn. In his three years at Highbury, Anderson had proved to himself that he could cope with the pressure of playing for a big club. He had gained confidence as a player and as a person and had been rewarded by his longest run as an England international. After a long apprenticeship, he was ready for the biggest club of all: Manchester United.

TEN

# GETTING SPLINTERS

The World Cup in Mexico in 1986 should by rights have been the highlight of Viv Anderson's international career. He had played in the notable victory against Russia and against Mexico in the warm-up matches. By common consent, he was playing better than ever in his twelve-year career. At the age of nearly 30, he seemed ready to face the ultimate international test. But slumped on the bed of his hotel room a few days before the start of the competition, Anderson must have felt an awful sense of *déjà vu*. A few minutes before, the England manager Bobby Robson had announced the team for the opening match against Portugal: Shilton, Stevens . . . Anyone who has ever been left out of a sports team, from the under-nines to an England international, will know the feeling; that strange combination of frustration, rage and helplessness which makes you want to stamp your feet and scream like a two-year-old robbed of a toy. Footballers have an expression for it, quite a good one: gutted. For the second World Cup running, Anderson was to be part of the squad, not part of the team. There is a huge difference.

'I was straight out of the team-meeting and up to my bedroom. My room-mate Terry Butcher had to put up with a terrible earful for the next hour or so. I was that desperate to play. The immediate reaction is to pack your bags and go home because all you've got to look forward to is sitting on the bench getting splinters in your backside for another month, and I'd already done that in the previous World Cup in 1982. But after a day or so, you just get on with it, whatever you feel inside. I was even more disappointed to be left out than in 1982 because I felt I had played well enough to be picked.

'It's harder for an international manager to choose a side than it is for a club manager because the differences between players are so much smaller. At club level, it's usually clear which one is the better player; at international level, that's not the case. Football is about opinion and the manager had to make a decision. I just thought he'd made the wrong one.'

There was more than just the disappointment of not being chosen for one World Cup match in Anderson's understandable but uncharacteristic show of frustration. His international career had not progressed with the smoothness forecast back in November 1978, when he sat on the team bus on the way to the match against Czechoslovakia listening to the experienced words of Bob Latchford. Since then he has played only thirty matches for his country. *Only?* Many – including, I suspect, Laurie Cunningham and Cyrille Regis who were both tipped to become England regulars at the same time as Anderson – would be happy with that number. But it ought to have been a lot more. At least that's what Anderson told me.

Footballers, however, are not generally regarded as the best judges of their own abilities. When things don't go quite according to plan, they tend to adopt the golden rule of the motorist in an accident: blame everybody in sight and never admit liability. Anderson is not so prone to that. He is defensive about criticism of his international record – partly because he reckons it's not too bad anyway, but mostly because he knows it could be a lot better and he cannot quite put a finger on why it isn't.

When he made his debut in 1978, the succession seemed secure. It was just a matter of how long Phil Neal's legs would last. But a few imposters got in the way: Trevor Cherry, Mick Mills, Mike Duxbury and then Gary Stevens. Only twice in his career has Anderson been able to say without fear of contradiction that the right-back position was his. The first was in the 1984-85 season when he enjoyed a run of six successive games as England qualified comfortably for the 1986 World Cup and the second was during another run of six games in the season after the World Cup as England qualified equally comfortably for the European Championships in 1988. He has the unusual but unwanted distinction of having been selected for two World Cups – 1982 in Spain and 1986 in Mexico – without playing a match. In 1980, he was in the England squad for the European Championships in Italy and played against Spain when England won 2–1, narrowly failing to qualify for the later stages.

There are plenty of good reasons for this halting progress, not the least of which is that, for a long time, Anderson did not reproduce his club form for England. In 1982, he had been selected for the England team to play West Germany at Wembley by the new manager, Bobby Robson, but the day before the match dislocated his right kneecap in training in a tackle on an unknown young winger called John Barnes.

It put him out of football for four months, out of international football for eighteen months.

'I think Viv has just been genuinely unlucky at international level,' said Don Howe. As England's assistant manager throughout most of Anderson's international career, Howe had to pick his words carefully. 'Perhaps he has been left out of the side on occasions when he didn't deserve to be. Maybe he just needed someone to tell him a little more often what a good player he is. During his later years at Forest, I think the edge went off his game and he lost his England place, but in the build-up to the World Cup he was one of our best players. There's not much to choose between him and Gary Stevens. I know who I would pick. Unfortunately, only one person's opinion counts.'

The question, 'Why can players who have played brilliantly for their clubs week in and week out suddenly perform like frightened rabbits for their country?' has been one of the eternal mysteries of life for England managers and, to a lesser extent, for the players themselves. Anderson agrees with Colin Bell, the former Manchester City and England midfield player, that it takes at least ten games to adjust to the pace and technique of international football. Players know the theory, they just find the practice rather harder than it looks.

'It's a bigger step than people think', says Anderson. 'You are supposed to go out and reproduce your club form at international level, that's why you've been picked. But it's very hard. The overall pace of the game is slower, the build-ups are more deliberate, you have to be able to put the ball on the spot nine times out of ten, not seven out of ten, and make it pay in key areas. It's a lot more clinical and you don't get second chances. One lapse of concentration and that's it – you've lost a goal or a chance has gone.'

There is no shortage of fellow travellers on the bumpy road to international security. John Barnes, transferred from Watford to Liverpool in the summer of 1987 for £800,000, has suffered more than most from the label 'inconsistent'. In a way, he had been the victim of his own brilliance. In ten seconds of blinding skill against Brazil in the Maracana Stadium, Rio de Janeiro, in June 1984, Barnes made a nation forgive his previous inconsistency, but he also raised the standards by which he would be judged in future. If he can dribble round half the Brazilian defence one minute, reasoned the terrace pundits, surely he can do it again the next. And if he doesn't? 'Well, I always told you he was inconsistent . . .'

'You can't just reproduce your club consistency,' Barnes said.

'There are league games every Saturday and if you have a bad match one week, you can always make up for it the next. At international level, however, there are so few games that if you play badly one match that's your chance gone for another three months, and if you play badly again that's maybe a whole six months. And if you play a good game, it's totally forgotten as soon as you have a bad one. Playing for a team like Watford – and this is no disrespect to them – you were not on top for a lot of the game and so you've not got the ball. That makes you seem inconsistent. At Liverpool, you are on top for most games, so you see a lot of the ball. There are no excuses for being inconsistent.

'It's better on an England tour because you know you are going to get two or three games to prove yourself and the games are often more relaxed. Not so much now, but a few years ago you could pick two England sides at the same time and not be sure who would win. What I find strange is that the press are always saying that so-and-so should be playing as if he is going to make the team worldbeaters overnight.

'It definitely would have helped if someone had said to me early on: "We'll give you four games to see what you can do." It would have made me more relaxed and more likely to play well. As it was, you knew you were always playing for your place and that was unsettling,' added Anderson.

Anderson also gets aggrieved about the power of the press in international selection, a view shared by Tony Woodcock, who also suffered from inconsistency of selection and of method. 'It was always difficult to become a regular international because of the pressure of the media. They shouldn't have any influence, but they do. Certain players get pushed in the newspapers and you need a manager strong enough to say, "This is my side", and then stick to it. That's probably why we weren't successful for a long period. It's different in Germany. When I was first at Cologne, we had five forwards but only two were going to play. It turned out to be Littbarski and me, which meant that Klaus Fischer was left out. Yet he still kept his place in the international side. That would never have happened in England.'

Like Anderson, Woodcock rarely enjoyed a consistent run in the England side and, as he wrote in *Inside Soccer*, when he did play, he invariably spent the game trying to win balls in the air or chasing long balls over the top. Neither suited his way of playing.

From near or far, Anderson has watched the development of the

England team over the past ten years. Not many have straddled the two World Cups or the two generations of England manager, Ron Greenwood and Bobby Robson. From the 1982 World Cup squad, seven players survived to play in Mexico: Peter Shilton, Ken Sansom, Glenn Hoddle, Terry Butcher, Ray Wilkins, Bryan Robson and Anderson. He has watched players like Lineker and Beardsley emerge, watched the period of change and consolidation under Greenwood bear fruition under Robson, watched results improve. In 1982, he first knew he had been selected for the World Cup squad when he heard it on the radio, while in 1986 the team virtually picked itself. 'In fact, so settled is the England side now that recently it has been like playing for your club at international level,' Anderson said. 'We all know the system we are going to play and what everyone else is going to do. That makes it easier for new players like Neil Webb because they are coming into a settled side and have time to find their feet.'

Despite the debacle of the 1988 European Championship, England's record under Robson is as impressive as any England manager of recent times and for that alone he must command respect. Articulate and endlessly enthusiastic, Robson was the natural successor to Greenwood after the 1982 World Cup. His great virtue is that he can judge good players, and the key to his record is that having done so he sticks with them. But, as the World Cup and the European Championship have shown, he can be guilty of astonishing tactical naiveté.

'He is lucky in that he has got good experienced professionals around him who can sort things out on the field if necessary,' is Anderson's view. 'But you can't get where he is, or have such a good international record, on luck. It's hard for any England manager to do well because of the strength of the club system, but he seems to be winning some battles in that the league programme was postponed before our European Championship qualifying match with Yugoslavia. Hopefully by playing so well that day we showed how important it is to have the right preparation for an international of that importance.'

Not surprisingly, as he selected him in the first place, Ron Greenwood holds a special place in Anderson's managerial hierarchy. 'He was a very nice man, never lost his temper, and was always considerate, ready to have a little word about your game and to explain why he wasn't picking you. He was amazed that I was an avid fan of *Coronation Street* – Debra tapes episodes I miss – and not long ago, when United went down to Weymouth to play a match to mark the opening of their new floodlights, Ron was there too, and he asked me, "Still watching *Coronation Street*?"

'The problem was that he wanted to keep everybody happy all the time. He wasn't really tough enough. For example, Shilton and Clemence playing in alternate games, that was typical of him; he couldn't make up his mind. He was at the opposite end of the spectrum from Clough. Clough wouldn't have had two people doing the same job. He would have made his decision and that would have been that.'

Anderson is not alone in thinking that, on merit, Clough should have got Greenwood's job when he was interviewed for it in the middle of Forest's Championship-winning season. But, even from this distance, it is easy to see why he didn't. After Revie's disgrace, the Football Association were first and foremost looking for someone to restore some honour to the job of England manager. Clough would not have been guaranteed to do that, at least not off the field. Moreover, the FA had appointed the most successful club manager in the land last time, and look where it had got them. Greenwood, with his West Ham background, his polite manner and his kindly face, fitted the bill perfectly. Clough, as Anderson says, never had 'a cat in hell's chance' of getting the job.

There could not have been a bigger contrast in the early fortunes of the England sides in Anderson's two World Cups. In 1982, England had qualified because Switzerland had obligingly taken three points out of four from Romania. They went to Spain on a wing and a prayer and surprised more than a few with their performances. In their opening match against France, they were a goal up in twenty seconds through Bryan Robson ('long throw-in, flick on by Terry Butcher, volleyed in by Pop,' said Anderson in a surprising display of total recall), won the match comfortably 3–1 and the group equally comfortably with maximum points. But, without Keegan and Brooking, they could not break down the defences of West Germany and Spain and failed to qualify for the semi-finals on goal difference. Their record – played five, won three, drawn two, lost none – was a comment on the ludicrous format of the competition. How, England supporters rightly asked, could you be knocked out of a cup competition without losing a match?

In Mexico, roughly the opposite occurred. England's results in qualifying and in beating Russia on their own territory had bred the view that Bobby Robson's side was at least semi-final material. But the opening two matches were disasters: defeat by Portugal and a draw with Morocco after Bryan Robson's suspect shoulder had finally given way and Ray Wilkins had been sent off for throwing the ball away at a free-kick. England's campaign was in tatters, as Anderson recalled.

'I remember watching the Portugal game with Peter Reid and he said at the time that we ought to be playing four in midfield. The problem for the first two games was that we were too strung-out. Portugal played five in midfield and, though we had a lot of the game, our three midfield players were getting run all over the place and our centre-halves ended up marking one man. You can't blame the manager, because the team we started with had played very well during the build-up. There was no doubt what way we were going to play, but desperate times require desperate measures, so we decided to change it.'

The 'we' referred to was critical in the post-World Cup analysis of England's performance. Who had made the change, the manager or the players? 'It was Peter Reid at a team-meeting before the Poland game. The manager might have been thinking the same way but it was clear to us that we had to play four in midfield and withdraw the front two a little so we were more compact. Peter Shilton or one of the other senior players chipped in and we all agreed with them. But, all credit to the manager, because it took some courage to change the side so drastically halfway through the tournament, though we couldn't do much worse than we had.' The rest, as Anderson would say, is history. The ball stayed on the floor, the two wide midfield players, Stephen Hodge and Trevor Steven, found the space to get round the back of the defences, and Lineker's remarkable instinct for goals – six in the next three games – did the rest. Only Maradona's hand stopped England's momentum and sent them back home earlier than the players felt they deserved.

After two World Cups, Anderson has had plenty of experience of the twilight world of the permanent sub, half glad because the team has won, half sad at not being part of the winning team. For a character like Anderson, who likes to be the life and soul of the party, the role was particularly difficult to handle. 'You don't really feel a part of it. After a game the players were allowed to go down and have a few drinks in the players' bar, but I tended to just have one and then go to bed.'

Ironically, no sooner had the World Cup finished than Anderson was back in the international team. In England's first match after that competition, Stevens was injured and Anderson returned to play possibly his best match ever for England. They lost 1–0 to Sweden, but Anderson stood out, as Bobby Robson acknowledged. 'Viv was the one real plus. He was terrific. He went through the World Cup without playing, yet was the life and soul in training. I was very pleased for him.'

Not surprisingly he kept his place for the next five matches, but ten years after his historic debut for England he was still not certain of his place for the European Championships in Germany.

Ironically, as he was joining the most prestigious club in the land, Anderson's move to Manchester United in the summer of 1987 did not help his chances. The change of club and the change of style initially did not suit him and he struggled to find his feet. He played against West Germany, but did not have a good game as England were beaten 3–1 and, halfway through the season, picked up a heel injury which plagued him for the rest of the season. Early in the summer of 1988, Anderson told the England manager that he would not be fully fit for the European Championships. Robson decided that Anderson's general *joie de vivre* was still worth a place in the squad and so for the third time in his career Anderson embarked on a campaign in which he was likely to play little part. In many ways, it was the most painful of the three.

High hopes were placed on the shoulders of the England squad. They had been together for a long time and had qualified more impressively than any other team in the tournament. An injury to Terry Butcher had made the centre of the defence look decidedly threadbare, but, with Lineker and Beardsley one of the most feared strike combinations in all the eight teams, the omens still seemed promising. But, as in Mexico two years earlier, everything went horribly wrong from the start. And this time, there was no third chance. Having been unluckily beaten in their vital opening match against Jack Charlton's Republic of Ireland side, England played well against the eventual champions, Holland, only to lose to three opportunist goals by the player of the tournament, Marco van Basten. They were out of the Championships and, to add to the embarrassment, were thrashed by the Soviet Union in their final match. No points, no pride, nothing to salvage from the wreckage either of the team's hopes on the field or the nation's reputation off it. Wherever England played, their supporters followed, leaving a trail of devastation in their wake. Both on the field and off, there were excuses, some valid, others less so. Yes, England had been unlucky – they hit the post twice against the Dutch; yes, their supporters had been provoked by German fans; no, there was little the Football Association could do to stop the trouble. Even so, it was a very sad England party that arrived back to face the criticism of the press. There were calls for Bobby Robson's resignation and polls conducted in the tabloids to find his successor.

Anderson was as perplexed as everyone else by the collective failure of the team and by the inability of individuals to live up to their past performances. Highest on that list was John Barnes. Anderson is a Barnes fan. It's only a matter of time before the nation sees the best of Barnes at international level, he says, but even he had to admit that the European Championships had almost passed Barnes by.

'Since he went to Liverpool he has been playing more like John Robertson used to at Forest. If he was being well marked he would play the ball off and create space for someone else and I thought England would benefit from that. But, like all wingers, his game is based on getting the ball. If he doesn't get it, you may as well forget about him. In the Championships, neither Barnes nor Waddle ever got a chance to run at defenders in the last third of the field. All Barnes's best work was done in the middle. He tends to feel he's having to chase full-backs the whole time when they should be chasing him. He got about two crosses to the back post in the whole tournament and Trevor Steven hit the bar with a header from one of them. The opposition pull people back in front of him and so he has to go hunting the ball in the middle which upsets the shape of the side. But, remember, he's still only 24, so as long as he can keep getting experience of international football, he will come good in the end.'

Being a loyal person at heart and therefore loath to criticize his fellow professionals, Anderson is more inclined to blame the English system than the players. But, as a product of that system and as a product too of Brian Clough, the manager most favoured on the terraces to manage England, Anderson's view, if not new, is based on experience.

'There is little you can do about several top players losing form at the same time. Perhaps we should have had more of a rest after the season, played fewer games and had shorter training sessions; that's being wise after the event. But, having watched the Italians, the Dutch and the Germans, it's clear that our formation and our style of play is too rigid. Rijkaard and Koeman, the Dutch centre-backs, could pop up anywhere on the field and not look out of place, but I couldn't imagine Dave Watson or Tony Adams going into midfield or going on a run down the right wing. That's down to upbringing. If our centre-halves at Forest went over the halfway line, Clough would go mad. They were paid to defend and that was it; he didn't want them disappearing off up the field all the time. We are suspicious of defenders who do that. Take Alan Hansen, for example. He's been one of the best defenders in our league for the past ten years and yet he's not in the Scottish side regularly.

'In international football, most of the front men and the midfield players are very tightly marked and nine times out of ten the only man spare is one of the two centre-backs. I thought the Italian sweeper Baresi was the best player in the tournament. In the game against Spain he suddenly turned up on the left wing. To be fair, we have had great success with the system we play, but we always seem to be found out at the very top level.'

Though rarely one to criticize team selection, Anderson could not understand why Hoddle was left out against Ireland. In fact, he can't understand why Hoddle has been left out of any of England's last 100 games. Hoddle, he reasons, is one of the few players that can match the continentals for pure skill.

'Glenn is one of the most gifted footballers we have ever produced in this country. If he had been playing for any other country, he would have had 100 caps easily by now. Yet we are suspicious of him. People say he is inconsistent for England, doesn't get himself involved enough, but I would have him in the team every time because of the service he can give to front-runners like Gary Lineker. He can put the ball exactly where he wants it from almost any distance, and that is a skill given to few footballers, believe me. I would play him just behind the front-runners where you need a bit of craft.

'Even hardened pros are amazed at his ability. In shooting practice, for example, inside of the foot, outside of the foot, left foot, right foot, he can hit them from anywhere. Sometimes, I can't believe some of the things he can do with a football, it's breathtaking. He has a reputation for being lazy, but I've never seen it. When he's played right midfield in internationals, he's always worked hard for me. The image he gives on the field is a bit arrogant and flashy, but he's not like that at all. He's quiet, sociable and very much the family man. I'd just love to see him playing in France because I doubt if the public believe that he's never been a regular England international.'

If you pushed him up against the wall, Anderson would admit that, after six years, it is time for a change of England manager, though he does not know who that would be. He likes Dave Sexton, but thinks he would be too much in the Ron Greenwood mould; he has heard good things about Howard Kendall from Peter Reid. And Cloughie? He'd love to see it, if only for the sport at FA headquarters.

Whatever happens, Anderson will not be part of the future. Shortly after the European Championships, Anderson announced his retirement from international football. It was a realistic decision, made quietly and finally, though not without regrets. 'I do feel I'm going out on a sad note. The international scene is looking very bleak because of the recent trouble. Everyone has to be depressed, but something's got to be done. I've got mixed emotions; on the one hand, with a bit of luck, I could have had fifty caps by now, on the other I have thirty more than I thought I would get. But I've had ten years of international football on and off and I've had a lot of European experience, which I am only starting to appreciate now. Besides, I'll be an old crock by the time the next World Cup comes round in 1990.'

ELEVEN

# ENGLISH BLACK, ENGLISH WHITE

In 1982, Anderson was offered £50,000 to play and coach in South Africa for a few months. He turned it down. The reason for revealing that fact is not to show that Vivian Alexander Anderson is on the side of Right and Truth in the crusade against apartheid, though I am sure he is, but that there is not one ounce of black radicalism in his eleven-and-a-half stone frame. He does not regard the refusal of the offer as important. He didn't even think of telling me about it until the last of our interviews and only then in response to a direct question about a previous visit to coach with Dave Sexton, Steve Heighway, Cyrille Regis and Gary Owen on a scheme sponsored by Mobil. He went to Soweto, did not like what he saw and did not go back.

'I talked to Clough about going. He didn't try to influence me either way, but in the end I felt it was not right,' said Anderson of the 1982 offer. He does not consider the decision a matter of honour or propaganda. It just seemed to be the right thing to do at the time.

If his colour has ever been a source of torment, self-consciousness or pride in his life, Anderson has forgotten about it. An early lack of confidence at Forest might have been due to the colour of his skin – Peter Shilton remembered him being slightly self-conscious about it – but equally it could have been due to a thousand and one other things: innate shyness, fear of Clough, of the senior players, of being a professional footballer, or just a lack of belief in his own ability. Anderson himself has stored away isolated incidents of racial awareness from his youth: a fight in the school playground, his first taste of racial abuse on the pitch during a reserve team game at Stoke, a mumbled compliment from another black player early in his career, warming-up as substitute with his back resolutely set against the terrace taunts of the Carlisle supporters, a television programme heralding the arrival of the black revolution before his international debut.

The dossier hardly points to a career fashioned by racial tension and driven by a desire to make a statement for the oppressed coloured community. 'If you're a black civil rights leader in Brixton, don't come to me. If I became involved in that it would be a false image of me. It wouldn't be the real me and I can't make myself something I'm not. I don't see any distinction between English black and English white. In Toxteth, Brixton or Tottenham they probably have grievances, but I've been lucky. My parents have always looked after me and my brother. But there is nothing false about me and it would be wrong for me to preach about this, that or the other when I've had no experience of it. Garth Crooks or John Fashanu are into that, but I'm not and I don't feel guilty about it. I know my limitations.

'Peter Taylor said I was the ideal leader of a black revolution in football when I made my debut for England. I never understood that. What am I an example of? Being able to kick a ball better than a lot of other people for ninety minutes on a Saturday afternoon, that's the limit of my example to people. The only reason I want to do better is for myself, not because I'm black or because people on the terraces are giving me stick. I want to become a better player and I don't consider my attitude a sell-out to my race. I am a footballer doing a job, so I want to do well for myself, my family, my manager and my team. That's all.'

The problem with that is, like it or not, a footballer does have influence quite outside his recognition. You only have to look at any under-nines match on a Saturday morning to see that. John Barnes would appreciate it too. He remembers watching Viv play for Forest on the television in the living room of his father's house in Jamaica. Unlike Anderson, Barnes is not inclined to play down the significance of being the first black to play for England, and as the first black player to make an impact on the traditionally white world of the Kop he can speak with some experience.

'It's not just a question of middle-class whites making a big thing out of it. It was a big achievement and should be recognized as such. When Viv made his England debut I was back in Jamaica and, at the age of just fifteen, I hadn't even thought of playing professional football, but for a seventeen-year-old coloured kid over here it must have been very important because it showed that it could be done. Now, particularly in London, every team has a number of blacks and if you look at the reserve team sheets at Arsenal and Chelsea, for example, there are almost as many blacks as whites. But, in Viv's early days, there weren't that many around so he would have made a tremendous impact.

'What is strange in Liverpool is that none of the black people in Toxteth have any interest in football at all. The black population is quite big – but Merseyside never had any black players so they don't identify with the game, whereas in London it's different. So when there was the banana-throwing incident in the match against Everton, people up here were astounded. Nobody could talk about anything else for weeks, but I got that in my first game for Watford against Chelsea so I got used to it. I suppose I should have done what Brendon Batson once did and stuffed the banana down my shorts. But I never worry about it. Never have done.'

From Stockholm to Upton Park, Carlisle to Parkhead, Anderson has had to put up with similar racial taunts from the terraces. Generally, he has ignored them, sometimes he has played up to them (when the notorious 'jungle' at Celtic jeered him as he came out on to the pitch for a UEFA Cup match, he took a bow), but never has he let them affect his play. Clough made sure of that early in his career. 'It's just the same as someone who's bald or got red hair. Terry Hennessy used to get slaughtered at Forest because he was bald. He couldn't do anything about that, just as I can't do anything about the colour of my skin. It's something I've grown up with, so it's never been a big issue. Having said that, I never found the racial prejudice that bad. I suppose if I had been playing for a London club at the time I made my international debut, it would have been a bigger deal, but coming from Nottingham made it easier for me.'

What upsets Barnes and Anderson far more than a handful of ignoramuses gaining amusement from hurling bananas and abuse is the stereotyped picture of the black footballer as a fast, instinctive and inconsistent forward. It is Anderson's great strength and perhaps his greatest legacy to the cause of black football that he only fits half that picture. He is fast and instinctive but he plays full-back, supposedly a position of responsibility and intelligence, and he happens to play with a devilish Anglo-Saxon consistency. If anything 'foreign' taints his game, it is a Latin tendency to harangue the referee and commit petty fouls.

'Black players have been accused of inconsistency,' he said, 'and players like Laurie Cunningham and Cyrille Regis have epitomized that. Perhaps that's why neither of them really came through to establish themselves at international level. But there have been countless white players who have faded away or taken a long time to establish themselves for the same reason – Peter Barnes, for one, Glenn Hoddle for another, and Colin Todd. He was the best defender I ever saw and he won less than thirty caps.

'I don't really know why the black revolution never really happened. Perhaps there were too many old-school-tie types at the FA. More likely, the players were simply not good enough. It was easier for me being a full-back: I was unique in that respect, others were forwards. All I was expected to do was kick a few people and go on the odd overlap and people would think I was wonderful. It's more difficult for a forward to be consistent.

'You look around now at players like David Rocastle, Paul Davis, Franz Carr, Des Walker and Chris Fairclough, and if they haven't become internationals in a few years' time, then you have to say that there's something wrong somewhere. There are so many more black players to choose from now – Regis, Cunningham and me were about the only ones around at the time. I can't believe that prejudice ever came into selection at any point in my career. Football is not like that. If you're good enough, you'll play.'

The truth is that Anderson fits the stereotype of the black footballer neither on the field nor off. His relationship with his parents is firm and respectful. He has always accepted authority, be it parental or managerial, and far from having a Rastafarian notion of 'let it be', he has inherited from somewhere a strong sense of the Protestant work ethic, which comes out on the football field as a rigid streak of professionalism. He sees his face in the mirror every morning without being aware of its colour, and professes views of self-help and individual enterprise straight from the Mrs Thatcher's book of Conservative capitalism. There is no notion of the hungry fighter in Anderson's background and it is to his eternal credit that he does not pretend that there is. Only in two ways does he conform to type: first, he didn't do very well academically at school because he was far too interested in sport; and second, he loves soul and blues music. Small consolations for the sociologist.

'I've never felt that I have had to strive that much harder because of the colour of my skin. I try to do a job to the best of my ability and, if good things come from that, then it's a bonus. I want to strive for better things and the only way I can do that is to play well every Saturday afternoon on the football field. I won't get them by being mediocre.'

The last word should perhaps come from Don Howe, who brought Anderson to Arsenal. 'The younger players all looked up to Viv, particularly the black kids like David Rocastle, Paul Davis and Micky Thomas. They don't know how lucky they were to have Viv there in their early days: first because he had time for the kids and second because he was a great mixer. They liked him and they learned from him and they could also say: "Well, if he can do it, I can do it too."'

TWELVE

# UNITED – FULL CIRCLE

There is every reason to believe that Anderson's guardian angel has a neat sense of order. How else can you explain the telephone call in the spring of 1987 which led Anderson away from one of the biggest clubs in the land to *the* biggest club in the land, the club that had rejected him as a schoolboy fourteen years before?

At the time of the call, Anderson had just enjoyed his most successful season with Arsenal. The team, brimful of talented youngsters, had taken the First Division by storm in the first half of the season and had won the Littlewoods Cup in the second. Under the forceful and disciplined leadership of George Graham, there seemed little doubt that they had begun a promising new era. Anderson's three-year contract finished at the end of July, but his experience and his example were badly needed to balance the club's youth, and not only did Graham have every intention of keeping him, but Anderson had every intention of staying. He and Debra had only just moved into a new house in Hertfordshire and the plan was to play out his First Division days in comfortable security at Highbury and then think again. But football does not deal in comfortable securities; the challenge of playing for Manchester United in front of 40,000 people and the incentive of a lucrative four-year contract proved too big an attraction.

Anderson's first meeting with United's top brass was unexpectedly comical. After the initial contact had been made, he was invited to meet the United chairman Martin Edwards and the manager Alex Ferguson. For talks that were supposed to be secret, the venue, the Albany Hotel in Nottingham, could not have been worse. Anderson arrived at the room booked for the meeting to find no sign of either Edwards or Ferguson. 'I waited for a time and then Martin Edwards sticks his head round the door: "Have you seen the manager?" he asks. "No," I said, "Well, I'll just go and find him," he said and off he went. A few minutes later, Alex Ferguson comes in: "Have you seen the chairman?" "Yes," I said, "he was in here a minute ago looking for you." "Right, I'll just go and find him," and he disappeared too. And I'm sitting in the room thinking, "What is going on?" It was a bit like a scene from *Fawlty Towers*, but eventually we all got together and I was very impressed with what they had to offer.'

There was only one final wrangle to be sorted out. How much was an England international full-back, aged thirty-one with boundless enthusiasm, considerable skill and dodgy knees, worth? Arsenal said £400,000, United £150,000. The tribunal decided £250,000, £25,000 more than the sum Arsenal had paid for Anderson from Forest three years earlier. At least the currency had not been devalued too much. So, at the start of the 1987–88 season, it was back to living in a hotel, back to commuting up and down the motorway, back to learning a new style of playing. At Old Trafford, it has never been a question of the ends justifying the means, the means were all-important too. A club brought up on the traditions of the Busby Babes, of Charlton, Best and Law were never going to accept mediocrity, whether it brought victory or defeat.

'The tradition does hang over the place,' said Anderson. 'You could see that when we had a minute's silence for the thirtieth anniversary of the Munich plane crash. Forty thousand people just went deadly quiet. It was quite remarkable. But you are expected to play brilliantly every week. If you are winning 1–0 with twenty minutes to go, the best thing to do is to make sure you keep a clean sheet and get three points. But at United they don't look at it that way. They'd rather you went out "Gung Ho" and then got beat 2–1. A brilliant game, but you've lost. I don't see it that way.'

Anderson had more problems adapting to the United style of play than he did at Arsenal. Arsenal always played to a system (it was sometimes a mystery which system it was, but it was a system none the less) but at United he found his football had to be less systematic, more off-the-cuff. There were no golden rules for defending and no room for the offside trap in United's football. Defending was something done when you weren't attacking.

'It took a bit of getting used to because things I was doing by instinct at Arsenal and Forest, I wasn't doing at United. I'd get the ball and find that my right midfield player was not where I thought he should be. Then I'd take too many touches and the ball would get intercepted. Little things like that. The more I played with the team, the better I got, but it was difficult to start with. I also hated living in the hotel; I like to have my things around me so the first few weeks until we got settled into our flat were a bit of a nightmare, to be honest.'

John Barnes found similar problems coping with the Liverpool style. 'I felt the same as Viv to begin with. I kept looking for the ball over the top and passes kept coming straight to me. At Watford, I just used to get past the full-back and sling in a cross. It was up to the forwards to get on the end of it. Graham Taylor would go mad if they didn't. At Liverpool, I did that and they said: 'Why cross that ball when there is no one in the box. Hold onto it and wait until someone gets there.' Well, of course, that was music to my ears. If I lose the ball in the meantime no one gets upset. If I'd have lost it at Watford trying to mess about, Graham Taylor would have gone mad,' said Barnes.

Apart from the different pattern of play, Anderson also found that Old Trafford was even more awe-inspiring than he had imagined. He had always viewed it as one of his lucky grounds. In his championship-winning year, a handsome victory at Old Trafford gave Forest a huge lift to their confidence at a vital point in the season; in his final season at Forest, he had scored against United at Old Trafford and again at the City Ground. Though he says he has long since forgotten the rejection in his youth, something about United has brought out the best in him. On the other side of the line, Anderson has found the pressures even greater than he thought. The club provided an Escort XR3i convertible – which had not been a perk of the job at Arsenal – and someone to look for houses and make appointments. Everything was done to make him feel at home. In return, though, Anderson felt that he had to do that little bit more for the club. 'You have to treat every game like a cup final here,' he said. 'Otherwise you will get turned over, and for a club like United that would be lethal.'

A poor first home match, ironically against Arsenal, plunged Anderson into the depths of despair, from which he and his confidence took time to recover. An international against Germany a month or so after he had arrived at Old Trafford did little to lessen his self-doubts. England were given a torrid time defensively in the first half and, to cap a bad night, deflections off his head and knee brought two German goals.

United too were still trying to find a rhythm. Injuries to Moses and McGrath weakened the backbone of the side and an experiment of using Bryan Robson as a sweeper did not work. While United were still trying to get into the saddle, Liverpool had galloped off into the distance, and by the time United began to give chase the title had vanished over the horizon. To complete an unsettled season for United, Alex Ferguson accepted the transfer requests of Whiteside and McGrath (the reported interest of Juventus in Whiteside causing the United dressing-room to erupt into cries of 'Juve, Juve' the following morning) though neither had left by the start of the 1988–89 season.

Despite the problems, United finished second in the league. Coinciding with his move to a new flat in the smart south-western suburbs of Manchester, Anderson's own form slowly picked up after Christmas, but even so he was not quite his old attacking self. For the last two months of the season he played with an injured heel, which finally had to be protected with specially moulded supports inside his shoes. He did not really take that into account when he summed up his first season: 'Average. I've not played too badly but I've not broken down any walls, either. I can play a lot better.'

Of course, he couldn't wait to be back to prove it. Despite nagging doubts about the foot injury which has refused to heal, Anderson has approached the new season, his second at Old Trafford, with the same touching combination of optimism and enthusiasm as he had the previous fourteen. With a new goalkeeper in Jim Leighton and the expensive combination of Brian McClair and Mark Hughes at the front, Anderson felt that 1988–89 might just be United's season. If so, his career would indeed have turned a neat, fulfilling and successful circle. But what happens when there is no new season to look forward to? The life of a top-class professional in any sport leaves little time for thoughts of the future, but anyway Anderson either cannot or does not want to contemplate life after football. His routine – down to climbing into a hot bath at 2.15 every Saturday afternoon, getting changed slowly at 2.30, not going out for a warm-up with the others, not going out on Thursday or Friday nights before a game – has been practised for so long, his concentration on his work so complete, that the routine of the outside world, like applying for passports and paying for hotel bills, has been largely shut out.

His wife feels the pressure of the future more than he does. 'He is so dedicated to his work that it will be frightening when it comes to that fateful day when he finishes. On the other hand, it might be a blessing because he will finally have time to look around and think what he is going to do. With what he is worth, he'll probably not have to work again, but I think he's frightened of how he might end up. What gives me great faith in him is that he likes to get up and get on with the day; I just hope that his enthusiasm will be transferred to something else.'

Anderson is clear what he *doesn't* want to do when his legs finally give out: own a pub or become a manager. He has had offers of work outside the game, but has made no firm decision about the future. He has built up a lot over the last fourteen years and with true Anglo-Saxon caution does not want to see it knocked down, but equally he is not about to break the habit of a lifetime by worrying unduly about it. If he could be given the gift of eternal youth, he would keep the same routine, enjoy the same friendships, the same excitement, the same despair, the same money, the same success. And that success has not been part of some rags-to-riches fairy tale; it has been much less romantic than that, a victory of determination, enthusiasm, discipline, and, in the precarious and neurotic world of professional football, for the plain and simple virtue of being a nice guy.